GOOD BOY ALCHEMY

Confessions of a White Cis Hetero Male

Nick Guthry

JETDA Books

Good Boy Alchemy
Confessions of a White Cis Hetero Male

This is a work of fiction. Several public figures and long-standing institutions are mentioned, but the story and the characters involved are wholly imaginary. The views expressed by the narrator and characters do not reflect the views of the author or publisher.

For more information, please address nickguthryauthor@gmail.com
or visit nickguthry.com

Issuer
Takanori Nagao

Publisher
Japan E-Book Technology Dissemination Association
(JETDA)
1-11-4-1000 Umeda, Kita-ku, Osaka 5300001
Telephone: +81-(0)-6-6131-8951

JETDA Publications issues ISBNs as an initiative to support publication. We are not responsible for the binding quality or the content of the work.

ISBN 978-4-86753-744-2
First edition 1 March 2024

Cover design by Chell Li

for the one in six

Man "possesses" many things which he has never acquired but has inherited from his ancestors. He is not born a tabula rasa, he is merely born unconscious. But he brings with him systems that are organized and ready to function in a specifically human way, and these he owes to millions of years of human development.

-Carl Jung

Foolish pride is what held me together
through the years

-Shawn Corey Carter

GOOD BOY
ALCHEMY

Part One

A Hoody
A Party
A Pamphlet

1

Children of Sin

2012

It is a Friday evening during September in the not-to-be-out-poshed neighbourhood of West Point Grey, Vancouver, British Columbia, Canada. Former Colony of the British Empire. Ancestral lands of the Coast Salish group of Squamish, Musqueam, and Tsleil-Waututh peoples. Earth, for readers of the far future. The sky is clear. The temperature outside is 10 degrees Celsius. And if you're not a smoker and you practice mindfulness, you can almost smell the Pacific Ocean of nearby Burrard Inlet. It is also the year 2012, which necessarily arouses all kinds of idiosyncratic associations in your silly human mind.

Now we are there, and we see John Foreskin, twenty-something-year-old, white, cis-hetero male, walking briskly down West 14th Avenue, a distinct hitch in his giddy-up. His sweaty hands are buried deep in his pockets. His shoulders are doing the work of the popped collar he is not wearing. And at first glance, we correctly infer a combination of nicotine, diuretics, and refined sugars. The continent among us feel an almost organic contempt.

Some twenty paces back at his millennial group home, John's peers in proto-adulting are gayly debasing themselves while the model-minority neighbours watch from their windows, wondering what's wrong, where the parents are, and why Caucasian youth seem to age so rapidly.

At the start of John's walk, he encounters some of them: well-to-do thirty- and forty-somethings, smugly toeing the line, fulfilling nature's prerogative, then signing up said prerogatives for extracurriculars. By all appearances, the children are in heaven, aloof to Gautama's diagnosis of the human condition.

I alone am at fault, he tries to convey with a meek smile as the mass of baseless pride lodged in his forehead embarrasses even the youngest of the children. They gawk while the parents can only usher them to the edge of the sidewalk, can only wonder what ungodly chance of nature could have spawned such a creature. John digs his hands even deeper into his pockets, trying to take up as little of the sidewalk as possible, determined not to light a smoke till he's at least off his own street.

If there is a track, he thinks, *their lives are on it.*

And yet…and yet this time there is no envy, if only because John Foreskin senses nothing magical about them. And John Foreskin, being a twenty-something millennial prone to mood swings, is all about magic. Whether magic is anything other than the caffeinated whimsy of youth is a question for another time, another phase of one's life.

He presses on, his pace brisk, and soon joins the hustle and bustle of West 10th. Lighting his first cigarette of the walk, he employs a steady, vacant gaze to accumulate several victories over people who make the mistake of underestimating him. Passing the yoga studio near Alma prompts the usual correction to his posture, and it occurs to him while looking in that he will probably never preside over the harem that his pedigree would have justified in bygone times. That his greatness is not immediately apparent to others accords with the discomfort he feels around men of greater height, strength, ability, and overall lifeforce. These encounters, by no means rare, interrupt, but do not extinguish, his sense of being somehow special.

He hangs a left on Alma towards West Broadway and Kitsilano, pushing through a crowd of UBC students waiting for the bus back to campus. He's sweating all over now, but it feels good, like he's on a mission.

On Broadway he passes a string of establishments boasting bars and grills, establishments where skirts are weaponized in the name of shaking what one's mother has given one, flaunting it if one has it, and paying one's rent and tuition. But the skirts never regard John the same way they regard the other cis-hetero male patrons, and John tells himself it's because he isn't daddy material.

Out on the patios, wheat-bellied daddies hush their wives to better hear themselves agree about the flatscreen play-by-play. In their eyes, past the satiated glaze, John discerns the inherited will to dominate, and concealed deeper still, the withering still-born form of the utterly dominated. Next to each pear-shaped patriarch sits the tragic tendency of the dominated to imitate their masters: at the sunburnt age of fifty-something, each wife lives trapped inside an uncanny impersonation of her husband.

Momentum next leads John past various hipster cafés where he knows he'd encounter more of his own kind: men hopelessly caffeinated and drowning in entertained possibility as they leak gasses barely visible to the human eye. These café types are higher-strung, more susceptible to dysentery and yellow fever (and every other ethnophilic fever), but otherwise brighter and better preserved than their inert patio cousins. The older ones remind John of what he needs to fear becoming, for with age their skittish momentum becomes more weakness than virtue. They have no business imbibing that much caffeine, let alone with milk and sugar. But they carry on as their bone density decreases and their inner cheeks discolour from the daily friction of violent wiping.

John knows swamp ass to be an epidemic in Vancouver, not just in his millennial group home, but nobody ever speaks of what goes on in the café washrooms. They walk in, never in a hurry, and walk out, however many minutes later, head held high, without ever once confessing the shame that has transpired, the shame that follows them back to their seats, that lingers in the bathroom waiting to accost the next visitor. The music and furniture encourage the delusion that this is Paris circa 1929, that one of the loose-bowled Xanders or Julians, by virtue of his name and tortoiseshell frames, is the next Sartre or Merleau-Ponty. Warmed-up croissants and for-here espresso cups help make it so. But it is all a lie. The sugar content of the cookies betrays the time and place as Post-Colonial Privilege, population: Children of Sin.

John feels the pull of the chewy molasses cookies, the warm lighting and plush leathers, the Barista's shy smile, but he pushes onward knowing that the ruggedness he longs for can never be achieved with sugar (crystalline levity) and protracted sitting in air-conditioned environments.

He veers off the main strip, and as the sun sets, the female baristas of Kitsilano breathe a collective sigh of relief. For now, they are safe from his prickly gaze. John is still twenty-something, lest we forget. He is still young enough to mistake his looks and vigour for signs of inner virtue. And he still assumes that women find his mix of eccentricity and inner torment attractive. He has not yet become aware of his particular brand of courtship—his latching on—and so has not yet become ashamed of it. In the coming years, certain encounters will give him the inkling that his schtick is passed expiry and that serious adult partnerships will require him to something more to the table. But that is far away now.

Almost home now, John Foreskin walks to extinguish self-consciousness, his audience at once everywhere and nowhere. He lights another cigarette and exhales into the cool night air. If no omen presents itself, he'll have to pass by the house, past the music and boozy chatter, and keep on walking until he gets that unmistakable feeling that the night has run its course. Down the back laneway, he kicks a stone and it hits the side of a garbage bin with a bang. A motion sensor light flicks on and he freezes. But that's when he sees it. The reason for his walk. Abandoned. An old exercise bike. He looks both ways. It's his now. Yes, he can lift it. And it's only ten or so meters to the house.

This is it.

It will be my outlet.

John Foreskin will sweat on his own terms now, long before he's ever left his bedroom, and then again after his final encounters of the day. He will have his own secret exercises, and the men of the house will wonder where all of his new vigour has come from. And the women will be the first to notice and the longest to look as his thighs transform into twin promises of stamina and virility.

He lugs the bike several metres then pauses, sweat streaming down his face. There's chatter coming from the house, but it's too faint to be coming from the back porch. Moving quickly, he lugs the bike into the yard, past the giant oak tree, then up the back stairs and into the kitchen. He stops again to catch his breath. He can hear his millennial associates out front, jabbering at high speed, and he prays to God and the Universe that none of them steps inside to witness the indignity of his labours.

After nearly falling down the stairs, he reaches the basement, unlocks the door to his bedroom, and drags the bike inside.

He has completed his quest. He is panting and more alive than he's ever been in his entire life. He tears off his shirt, then stands in front of his full-length mirror to confirm his self-image.

2

Thank You, Tenderness

2022

Let us jump ahead now, approximately ten years. Vancouver is blessed with another beautiful spring day., and John Foreskin and his FTLIJGF[1]—who is a fully autonomous being unto herself—are returning home from a nice walk in the neighbourhood of Marpole.

As they approach their apartment building, John Foreskin is aware of their approaching the apartment building; moreover, he is engaged in a mental visualization of their approach, including a distinct notion of how he looks as well as how he and his FTLIJGF appear as a couple. Arguably if not obviously, this is not an activity that John need engage in to complete the

---

[1] Full-time live-in Japanese girlfriend

task at hand, let alone survive, i.e. his continuing existence as a human being is not contingent upon his continuous visualization of his existence as a human being.

Abstractions within abstractions:

In John Foreskin's reproduction of his life, audience John, he looks at himself as his self of twelve months ago would have looked at himself: envious. He and his FTLIJGF are en route to their sky mansion,[2] and John of Today is looking anything but his old gaunt self, anything but the hard-done-by variety of white-man millennial on the verge of racism, sexual violence, and/or anti-vax freedom convoy.

We've already inferred how things very quickly get racial for John, Caucasian as he is.[3] So we are not at all surprised that it is buckshot to the gut for John of Twelve Months Ago to see John of Today entering his swanky-ass apartment with a younger Asian female, plus the fact that it is nearly noon on a weekday and that both John of Today and his hand-in-hand rice cherub are rosy-cheeked from having walked against the wind on a brisk spring day. All of this conveys to John of Twelve Months Ago (unshaven and disenfranchised) that this power couple enjoys a worry-free life-

---

[2] High-rise apartment

[3] cf. Kendi, Ibram X.; DiAngelo, Robin J.

style of leisure, financial security, and consensual intercourse.

John of Twelve Months Ago has every reason he now needs to hate god, the world, capitalism, men he doesn't know, the extroversion of salespersons, most men he knows, his lack of resolve, the sun for making him sweat, financially independent women for scoffing at his poverty, the wind for exposing his hairline, loud cars, certain people from his past, the news media, the gumption of youth, the happy, and his own life—every reason to retreat to his basement hovel, hate and avoid his pathetic-excuse-for-a-human-being, middle-aged, obese, balding, male roommate, order Uber Eats, overeat, and then tunnel what dim consciousness remains into a Twitch stream of a 25-year-old PC game played by a 35-year-old who is even more of a degenerate than John Foreskin of Twelve Months Ago is himself.

All that John of Twelve Months Ago now sees is a man who has in his possession all that *he* wants. But only John of Today is aware of all the worries he carries, the worries that John of Twelve Months Ago would never even suspect. The aforementioned entering of the swanky-ass apartment building hand-in-hand with his in-all-likelihood too-young girlfriend of Asian descent has not rendered John of Today's life worry-free. On the contrary, now that John of Today has fulfilled his two primary goals from twelve months ago—living in his own apartment and having an Asian girlfriend (the latter most certainly betraying him as a racist misogynist)—John of Today is faced with a new set of worries, worries that could only have come with his newly colonized territory: maintaining the peace between himself and his girlfriend, and affording the rent of his new apartment.

Thus, John of Today waits for the elevator feeling all kinds of imposter syndrome, for he now projects onto every other resident a worry-free, financially secure existence. He assumes, moreover, that each one owns not rents, that they have a career they feel great about and an active social life, including a group of friends they go hiking with on the weekends. In other words, despite John of Today's recent levelling-up, his default posture is the exact same as that of John of Twelve Months Ago, twelve years ago, twenty-four years ago: envy—envy sustained by the uninterrogated premise that the lives of others are unequivocally better than his own.

However, what John of Twelve Months Ago and John of Today both fail to consider is that each has fewer worries than John of Thirty Years Ago. And that is because each John has, as of some five years ago (or four, depending on the John), divested himself, at least partially, of the long-lingering shame of his first predatory encounter.

So, of course, Little John of Thirty Years Ago, knowing only that a certain secret must be kept and expending no small part of his lifeforce on keeping it—first consciously and then subconsciously—was living a more stressful life, his expression stifled, his being disconcerted, as he bore the burden that neither Adult John would dare reassume, nor wish upon his worst enemy.

It is this epiphany, and the ensuing empathy for Little John, that finally frees John Foreskin of Five Minutes Ago from his adulting-under-capitalism malaise. The cup suddenly feels half-full again, and as he sips his post-walk coffee, yesterday's brew cold from the fridge, he thanks the Universe for tenderness, much the way Alanis Morissette of Twenty-Four Years Ago thanked India.

3

Caucasian Millennials

2012

Our intrepid twenty-something millennial is out for another no-nonsense walk, his destination: the Starbucks on the corner of West 10th and Tolmie. The sun is shining, and gratitude suggests itself as a potential state of mind, if not spontaneously via the heart chakra, then rationally, via abstraction, and the inevitable conclusion that to be alive and well, here in Vancouver, is to be better off than innumerable other human beings on planet Earth.

Heavy sigh.

John Foreskin fingers the pack of Belmonts in the front pocket of his made-in-Sweden red canvas pullover hoody before stuffing his right hand back in its rightful pocket.

For reasons relating to chadhood and Brad Pitt circa *Fight Club,* he has committed to having his first cigarette of the day only after getting his first light-iced grande almond milk latte. Delaying nicotine will allow the sun to have her way with him, at least until he reaches the café. John could tell you all about how the sun punishes those who have lived the previous night as if it were their last, or as if *there were* no last, as well as those who seldom increase their heart rate through exercise, plus also the hyper-glycemic who require a sugar fix after every micro-aggression and crowded elevator ride. And John Foreskin knows he falls into at least two of these categories. But at least he exhausted himself last night on his new exercise bike.

Based purely on the number of stay-at-home milfs entering and exiting the boutiques along West 10th Avenue, we can determine the time of day to be around eleven o'clock in the morning. We can then, based on this premise, make further deductions about John Foreskin's lifestyle.

As he navigates the sea of strollers and Lululemon tights, a melange of pheromones and perfumes insinuates into his already sweaty loins. The milfs know that he only rents, that he's an imposter in this neighbourhood. And John knows that, in their eyes, his astounding virility will never compensate for his obvious inability to navigate adulthood. Their knowing smiles refer not to any joie de vivre, nor to the beautiful autumn weather, but to John's twenty-something precarity, and to the most recent time he sullied himself with masturbation. His protective reflex is to tunnel his vision and stuff his hands even deeper into his pockets, depriving his armpits of any oxygen, and his arms of any movement, they might have naturally enjoyed. The sun beams down as his sweaty, unscaped catholic area becomes a more prominent abstraction in his mind, as his skull becomes, more definitely, the outer limit of his consciousness.

Up ahead, a dark figure emerges from the Starbucks and pauses thoughtfully before turning toward John. As John approaches, a knowing nod is the most his inner little boy could have hoped for and is more than enough for his stern, grown man.

The figure is le Kyle, Sa'ad le Kyle, John's ethnic housemate (They/Them). In another lifetime, they might have been a pirate, in yet another, a sultan. Their skin is the rich mocha-brown that sees Caucasian millennials contemplate interracial marriage. They are gloriously human in their tank top, their brow in perpetual repose, their hairline the epitome of honesty. The sun seems only to approve of them.

"Sup."

"Foreskin! What are you saying? I feel like I always see you here."

"I know, right? Latte?"

"Cappuccino."

"Nice."

"You going in?"

"Yeah."

"I'll wait for you. My drink's too hot anyways."

A seamless exchange. And he was addressed as *bro*. John feels as if these encounters happen often, and that when they do, they confirm he's on the right path in life. Especially when caffeinated, nicotated, high, or tipsy, John Foreskin favours explanations involving karma and following one's heart. *Co*-incidence, cold and barren, does nothing for him. Scientific material-ism, as a paradigm, feels likewise unsatisfactory, though he avoids talk of 'vibes' when in the company of two or more Caucasians.

He enters the Starbucks and immediately scowls at the stagnant air, plus anybody who may have turned to look at him. He meets no eyes. He screws up his own so as to see the world without actually *seeing* the world. He stumbles through his order but accepts this as evi-dence of his candidness and the scatterbrained, bed-head delirium that the right kind of girl will find en-dearing. None of the usual baristas are working today though, at least nobody that he feels is definitely his type. The present moment, therefore, serves only as a precursor to the first sip of his latte and his first drag of nicotine, and he cannot afford to be *present* in it. In less than five minutes, he exits the café, iced latte in hand, and joins le Kyle in lighting a cigarette.

The first exhalation unites the two millennials in an interracial siblinghood of consciousness. Their first sips evoke gratitude for life and do more to dispel nihilism than a two-hour Jordan B. Peterson talk. It's 2012 though, so neither lost boy has even heard of JP yet.

"Hold on," says le Kyle. "Dmitry keeps texting me."

"The new guy upstairs?"

"Yeah, " le Kyle says cheerfully. "You met him yet?"

"We only talked a little. Seems cool though. Russ-ian?"

"Yeah. Grew up in Saint Petersburg. He and I go way back. But yeah, what'd you get up to last night? Drink any?"

"Yeah. Kinda feeling it to be honest."

"Same, bro. Plans for tonight?"

"We'll see, I guess."

"Walk and smoke?"

"Alright."

"Where to, Mr. Foreskin?"

"Wherever, man. I'm down for anything."

Le Kyle takes the lead, and John finds comfort in deference. As they stroll around West Point Grey, their cigarettes garner approval from pre-Karen milfs who have ventured out to undo some of their domestication by basking in reassuring amounts of male gaze.

After John's third drag, his body is insulated by a sedating yolk, beyond which nothing of the world is sufficiently threatening or appetizing to fully register. He catches le Kyle's eye, and they share another nod. John learned empirically, years ago, that the sun won't stop having her way with him until he's a few drags into his first cigarette of the day. Once he is though, he becomes something of a Russian ballet dancer. Graceful. Taut. Virile to the nth.[4] He counts this as a fact of life that does not require corroboration from a single other human being.

A pack of probably-Chinese, probably-university students appear down the street, heading towards John and le Kyle, probably for the Starbucks. Things always get racial, and fast, for John Foreskin, Caucasian as he is. The students are clad uniformly in black, oversized luxury-leisure wear. Their leather loafers and backpacks are studded with spikes of gold and silver. Cropped pants bare their hairless ankles to the world. From the security of their group, they emit

---

[4] Where $n \geq$ the virility of Andrew Tate circa 2023.

guttural laughter and a coarse mega-city dialect into the atmosphere.

John scoffs, desperate for some kind of acknowledgment and unable to bear their apathy. His cigarette, his iced latte, le Kyle by his side—all are assets. As the pack approaches, he delays his next exhale ever so slightly. Then, locking eyes with the lead boy, he exhales dragon-style through his nostrils.

He immediately regrets the maneuver. The boy's cynical, droopy gaze does not waver, and John is first to look away, sniffing sharply upwards to save face.

More laughter as the pack passes. Their contentment persists, despite the sun, despite the world. Where John struggles, sweating, straining, they seem only to drift like clouds, insulated from anxiety by monthly allowances and daily bubble teas. Their youth offends him. Their women tempt him and mock him, in that order. Their insularity baffles him.

How do they—?

How is it that they—?

John Foreskin takes another drag of his morning Belmont. Sheer majesty. And then it suddenly becomes so clear. Yes, he can feel it: the boundary of their extroverted veneer, past which is to be found their tender, resounding offence. For they can always take offence, as soon as a certain line is crossed. And their parents will sort things out by way of a new apartment, a new car. With money comes a certain facility that can sometimes pass for equanimity, a facility that ridicules John's precarious, caffeinated shambles. John has none of this facility. But of course that hasn't stopped him from buying Starbucks on a daily basis for what feels like years now.

He takes another drag of his Belmont then skips to catch up with le Kyle on the crowded sidewalk. They pass Liberty Wine Merchant, Top Ten Produce, and Claire's on Tenth, the artisanal cheese shop where one of their ex-housemates worked before she got pregnant and moved in with her boyfriend.

As John sips his latte, he reflects on the intersectionality of his race and generation:

```
          c
          a
          u
          c
          a
          s
    m  i  l  l  e  n  n  i  a  l
          a
          n
```

Most, having left the nest, are neither beholden to nor financed by their parents. They flutter from perch to perch, various student houses and basement suites, until they've concluded their mandatory experimentations with veganism, social justice, neo-paganism, and polyamory. Such is the stretch of arrested development between the end of high school and the unplanned conception of the first hyperglycaemic, ADHD-prone child.

John looks back in time to see the pack of Asians entering the Starbucks. Even the bad boys among them ooze a kind of conventionality that a part of him envies, and that he correlates directly with their tendency towards juvenile hairlines. Compared to them, he feels somehow experimental, off the rails and delinquent. He is no less ashamed of his whiteness in front of them than he is in front of le Kyle or any other legally recognized ethnic group of colour.

"Easy, bro." Le Kyle grabs John's shoulder just as a minivan whizzes by. "Didn't you see the light?"

"Fuck. My bad."

Their hand still rests on John's shoulder. "You good?"

"I'm good. I'm just...a bit stuck in my head I suppose."

"I'm like that half the day, man. I should probably meditate, or something."

The light changes and they start crossing.

"I'll send you a YouTube video on meditation," says John, pleased at having something to share. "You might enjoy it."

As they reach the curb, their eyes lock, and for a split second John sees himself in le Kyle's face, his European features superimposed onto le Kyle's mocha-brown skin.

Something inside both of us—

It's…the same.

The bond quickly becomes too much for either bro to handle, and both look away at the exact same time.

"I—I gotta go—blow off some steam," stammers John, failing to properly flick his smoke.

"Yeah man…" le Kyle says with a gulp. "You do you."

John is already marching off in the direction of UBC, wearing a consternated frown that he associates with honest self-reflection. Le Kyle's soft eyes rest on his red hoodie a while longer.

4

The Basic Formula

2012

The wholesome phase is over with. You've been smoking too much. And you never really exert yourself physically, do you? Now, a single double-quarter pounder BLT with cheese will be the gateway to an entire week of reprobate consciousness, totally disconnected from the silent truth you've glimpsed so many times now. Sunlight exposes semen stains on the hardwood floor.

No! Fuck you. You've made the right choice with this walk. Halfway through, it will turn into a run because you've worn the right shoes for it and because it doesn't matter who sees you sweat.

No! Fuck YOU. The soft way is a way. No need to strain. Go home. Take the afternoon easy. Just don't fall into masturbation so easily.

No! FUCK YOUUU. The pendulum has swung, hard. Binge and purge, bitch. Binge and purge. Besides, retaining that much semen is bad for your prostate. You could literally die if you don't masturbate right now. Go home and do it now! There's no such thing as a god who is watching you. That's just your pathetic attempt to police yourself.

John Foreskin has been speed walking for forty-five minutes. He finished his iced latte within seconds of parting from le Kyle and tossed the cup in some bushes because fuck the burden. He hasn't touched his Belmonts since, but his stomach feels upset from the latte before breakfast (as if he hasn't already learned that lesson a thousand times). As usual, he has no idea where he is, nor any particular destination in mind. He presses onwards, hands pocketed, eyes fixed on the stretch of sidewalk ahead. On residential streets, he recognizes the familiar urge to look into the windows of passing houses, to taste the various kinds of family life. In his present mood, it strikes him as utterly craven.

What happened back there?

With le Kyle.

His phone starts buzzing up his pocket. He whips it out mid-stride.

A text from le Kyle:

Bro,
I lost Kerry's number
Do you have it?
Also, hope that walk is helping

Then another message:

Also, send me that meditation vid later?
Peace

Kerry is one of their housemates. Cis-gender female. Solidly 5′7″. Bio major with a minor in Psych. Caucasian to the bone. She was also Canadian national chess champion for girls under seventeen and currently plays board 4 for UBC.

John has no choice but to give le Kyle her number, not that he can think of a reason not to.

A girl, maybe fifteen, approaches on the sidewalk wearing a hoody and denim cut-offs. Winter's pale lingers on her thighs as if she went all Summer thinking she couldn't pull them off. Several paces behind, a large, bearded man walks a German Shepherd.

"Pasta tonight sound okay?" he calls ahead, fatigue in his voice. "With Caesar salad."

"I had pasta at Mom's last night," the girl retorts. "And we always have Caesar salad."

The girl and the dog both smile and John offers a tight-lipped nod. But the man's eyes are filled with suspicion as if John just committed a crime.

A few blocks later. A busier street.

Finally. Is this King Edward?

No?

Why do I never know where I am?

Then John sees it. A Starbucks up ahead, like a desert oasis. It's odd though. A handful of people seem to have gathered outside. As he approaches, a man's voice becomes audible:

 "The human mind is composed of p*eek*chures of your life, taken with five senses and stored in your body. The human body, my friends, is a camera."

John posts up against a telephone pole and lights a smoke. At first glance, the man reminds him of a Soviet-era grandmaster: suit and tie, pomaded hair, childlike blue eyes embedded in a severe face.

"With five senses, we record every moment of our lives. And then, we live inside recording. That," he says, pronouncing it *zat*, "is how we construct our realities. That is where we find sense of self, yes? But *where* could we say that self exists?" The man pauses, eyebrows raised, and looks around the audience. "*Only* in your mind," he continues, his eyes landing on John. "Only in your mind."

John holds the man's friendly gaze.

"And who knows all about that self?" he continues, clearing his throat and returning to the others. "*Only* you do! *Sozen*, my friends, in what sense can we say self exists?"

A couple close to the speaker shuffle off, smiling politely.

The man continues, unfazed. "To be truly free, to be truly *alive*, that false self *must* be destroyed! Along with the pictures body has accumulated. We must keep *subtracting* the human mind until only the pure universe remains. *Then* we will know our true selves. *Then* we will be living in the real world."

The Universe.

Something deep inside John flinches at the use of that term.

The man grins, exposing crooked teeth, and begins handing out blue pamphlets. John flicks his smoke and ducks inside the café.

There's no lineup and he immediately orders a second light-iced grande almond milk latte along with the Everything Croissant Ham and Egg Breakfast Sandwich, his go-to for when his gut needs something to work on. He pays with his Mastercard.

The sandwich is heavy, and he eats it too quickly. He can feel a premature bowel movement coming on now.

Luckily the café is practically empty, just a few Boomers barely managing to work their devices.

Buzzing in John's pocket.

A text from Corey:

Bro, meet up?
I'm near the park at Dunbar.

Corey is one of John's leftist friends. He's read Noam Chomsky, but also Sam Harris. He majors in History and minors in Philosophy (John's major). Corey takes part in railroad blockades to oppose trans-mountain pipelines. His environmentalism also entails veganism, not flushing if it's only pee, and dumpster diving. He knows le Kyle and pretty much everyone else in John's house. (It's common knowledge that he used to have a crush on Kerry.)

John knows that meeting up with Corey means blazing. He's fine with that, but he'll need to evacuate his bowels first. He isn't about to get high at some far-off park when he's practically crowning.

Five to seven minutes later: the load was reasonably solid, suggesting vigour and sexual continence on John's part. He then approves of his reflection in the mirror. Examining his hair, his thoughts turn to le Kyle and earlier.

He probably thinks I'm weird now.

Why would he need Kerry's number?

Unless…

He inhales deeply, gives himself one final look, then exits the washroom.

On his table, standing right next to his iced latte, is a blue pamphlet. He looks around the café. It's the same crowd as before. And none of the other tables has one. He picks it up:

Find your true mind: The Universe Mind
The Method
Free Introductory Seminar

The pamphlet is filled with photos of happy people, very clean-cut, with deliberate ethnic heterogeneity. On the back, there's a stick figure drawing that John feels strangely drawn to without even knowing precisely what it's supposed to be depicting.

He looks around once more before sliding the pamphlet into the front pocket of his red hoodie. Then he picks up his latte and exits the café.

The pomaded man is nowhere in sight. The sun is shining, and John lights his third cigarette of the day, fully justified by the shameless bowel movement. Then he whips out his phone to confirm his route. The park is about ten blocks away.

Let's fucking do this.

As his body heats up, he recalls Drake's hook from that one DJ Khalid song. He definitely feels *on one* right now, where being *on one* is defined as having activated one's mojo, where mojo is in turn defined as that pre-lingual faculty that steers one towards irrevocable chadhood. He counts the shameless bowel movement as evidence, not to mention his impromptu trans-ethnic encounter with le Kyle and the follow-up text message. Now, meeting Corey in the park feels like fate.

Fuck it. I'm on one.

◆

"Coffee beans don't grow anywhere in the industrialized north."

"Truth."

"And so the pale-skinned, sun-wary capitalist patriarchs must import them."

"To carry out the rituals demanded by their productivity gods."

"Precisely."

"And then to imbibe the resulting fluid."

"Correct. They imbibe the resulting fluid, and then, under the influence of its brief spell, maximize capitalist-colonialist productivity."

"And the final rite takes place in a washroom, does it not?"

"Correct again. It's in the washroom where they... divest themselves, of the spell's resultant quasi-solids."

"And the shame disappears into the network of hidden pipes below our paved cities."

"Yes! As we suffocate Mother Earth with our concrete. And people wonder why I prefer to meet up in parks. *Honestly.*"

"Most of the shame anyways."

"You want any more of this?"

"I'm good, bro."

Corey scrutinizes what's left of the joint. "Any idea *why* le Kyle changed his pronouns, by the way?"

"You mean *their* pronouns?"

"My bad. *Their* pronouns."

"Haven't asked. We chilled earlier today though. Starbucks run."

"Oh really?" This information is sufficient to raise Corey's right eyebrow a full centimetre. "Very nice. He's—they're—such a solid dude—person, I mean."

"Indeed."

Corey enters a fit of coughing.

"You alright, man?"

"I'm fine, he says, eyes watering. "Fuck I love cau-
liflower."

◆

The sun is low in the sky. John Foreskin power walks,
hands pocketed, in the general direction of his millennial group home.

Blazing went as expected, though he found himself
growing impatient every time Corey held the joint for
too long, not to mention vaguely put off by his Bob
Marley beanie.[5] Afterwards, he declined Corey's invitation to watch a documentary about aliens and pyra-
mids.

"Fuck. I'm too high. Why do I always—." But he
stops, feeling silly for talking to himself out loud.

The cars whizzing by are invariably occupied by
sober, extroverted, goal-oriented adults who see plainly
that something's not right with John.

Just make it home. The walk will help.

He sticks to the main roads, avoiding eye contact
with other pedestrians.

What's with me today? Why was I so upset this morning,
in front of the Starbucks?

---

[5] Subconsciously, Corey believes that his veganism gives him
carte blanche to appropriate Rastafarian culture.

Am I racist?

How can I be? Le Kyle's my bro—I mean…

Why did they change their pronouns anyway?

Probably not something I should ask.

I wonder what Kerry thinks.

Today was fun though… He—They—saved my life!

John touches the shoulder where le Kyle caught him at the intersection, remembering that moment between them, how his features looked positioned under le Kyle's hairline.

That's it!

They were…

It was…

An invitation..?

Yes!

But also…

A challenge…

A challenge?

"A challenge!"

John trips but manages to break his fall. Before he can stand up, a group of teenage boys turn the corner.

"You stoned, buddy? I almost ran into you."

"This fucking white boy's stoned as fuck, yo. Look at his eyes!"

"My bad. I'm good," says John, standing back up.

And you're white anyhow! So what the fuck?

"Muyy beddd!"

"I'm *ggood* dawg. I just tripped!"

"Bah*wa*hahaha." The boys erupt, falling over each other.

"Not tripped, my guy. Tripp*ing*. Tripp*ing*, you heard?"

Stop talking Black! Jesus Christ.

"What the fuck is this?" one of them announces, snatching the pamphlet from John's hoody.

Fuck.

"Find your true mind: The Universe Mind," the boy reads in a sultry voice. "Bro, what the fuck?"

"This is some cult shit. You tryna' recruit us?"

"Who the fuck cares. Let's go."

The boy holds out the pamphlet, and John snatches it back.

They walk off, still chuckling.

"Get home safe, bro. And lay off the weed, okay?"

John stuffs the pamphlet back in his front pocket and starts walking.

A distant shout: "I'm *ggood* dawg!"

More laughter.

Fuck off!

They wouldn't say shit if le Kyle were here.

They'd be too ashamed.

John Foreskin lights another cigarette.

There was real brotherhood this morning.

Siblinghood. Whatever.

No fake fucking "buddies."

But…But what was it that le Kyle was trying to tell me?

John grasps his forehead, massaging his temples.

Wait! That's it!

His eyes widen.

If I can somehow master myself and…

And what?

And get things back under control so that…

So what?

So that my hairline returns to its juvenile position! Then…

Then what? And get what under control?

Then le Kyle would no longer count me as one of the white boys they knew…I would become his — their — brother!

You're too fucking high right now.

No! It's not crazy. I can transcend my race by…

By correcting my v-shaped hairline!

Yes!

The punishment given to our ethnic group for…

For our excesses of cunning during the colonial period of recent centuries!

Yes!

Nicotine floods his legs and he staggers, catching himself on a telephone pole.

Am I talking to myself right now? Or am I talking to Corey, inside of my head?

Hence the bulbous foreheads and V-shaped hairlines of so many cartoon supervillains!

In movies, too!

Exactly! They're…they're angry at God for their lot in life and are always hatching cunning plans.

Yes! Cunning plans are hatched in the forehead, specifically in the temples!

That it! That's always been the way.

You're too high right now.

No! It's true. I've always known it. I came into this world knowing it. It's…

It's the Basic Formula.

The Basic Formula, recognized by John since before he could walk *or* talk, and adopted—nay, inherited—according to John's calculations, by at least 75% of adult males, and not just Caucasians. The Basic Formula:

- To let pride down past the brow feels like losing

while

- To retain things there and accumulate even more feels like winning

Then, right on cue, a line pops into John's head:

Brow backed up with old accounts
Hating God with every ounce

Oh my god! That poem…from…?
He clutches his head again.
Where do I know those lines from?
A couple approaches on the sidewalk, mid-thirties, walking a Terrier. They stare at John who's still leaning against the pole. He forces himself to start walking again.
They know!
Know what?
They know what I'm carrying in my forehead!
The Terrier starts barking and John nearly shits himself.
The dog knows! Animals can sense things!
The couple glares at John with twisted, derisive smiles, inducing the impulse in him to sniff upwards sharply into his forehead.
Stop that! That's— That's saving face! That's the formula at work!
With every fibre of his being, he resists.
Remember, even when nobody else knows, the Universe still knows. The Universe always knows!

Brow backed up with old accounts
Hating God with every ounce

Why do I feel this way?

Don't you know? It's the price you pay for the imbalance of accounts! This is why mornings are so difficult, and why the Sun always merks you. The sun is Nemesis, Greek goddess of divine retribution.

Yes! She is punishing me for my hubris!

The hubris you're keeping in your forehead!

I'm way too high right now...

John finally turns onto West 14th. The living room lights are on in the house. His mind conjures an image of le Kyle and Kerry making out on the couch, Kerry unbuckling le Kyle's belt as she runs her other hand through his luscious locks.

Why would they need her number unless...

He reaches the house but keeps walking towards the pink horizon.

Brow backed up with old accounts
Hating God with every ounce

That's it! That big book of poems!

It was the very last one!

It's probably still—

He stops at the corner, whips out his phone, and e-mails his mom about the book. With any luck, it'll be on the bookshelf in her condo.

He pockets his phone and squeezes his eyes shut. Tighter, tighter, leaving his senses behind. His mind gradually quiets. And then he feels it, the rush of the darkness. He doesn't fight it. He surrenders. And it swallows him whole.

The world disappears.

His body fills with energy.

His body disappears.

John Foreskin disappears.

And for a moment, there is oneness.

And then, from that silent emptiness, the thought emerges:

The Universe.

John opens his eyes. The sun has set. He pulls out the pamphlet.

Find your true mind: The Universe Mind
The Method
Free Introductory Seminar

Is it a cult?

And what did that man mean exactly, when he said 'the Universe'?

John keeps walking until the munchies finally set in. Then he turns on his heels and heads back to the house.

5

Ressentiment

2012

Caffeine figures heavily in the plumbing of 4474 West 14th and its millennial tenants.

The basement and main floor share the full bathroom opposite the living room. There is also a shared bathroom on one of the upper floors that John Foreskin has never used nor whiffed nor peeked inside of. He's only ever used the back staircase down to the basement and couldn't even tell you for sure how many floors the house has. What he does know is that le Kyle lives alone on the loft level with their own full bath, an arrangement that John understands to be a kind of retroactive ethnic justice.

In the names of proto-adulting and productivity, most tenants drink coffee and/or espresso daily, while Red Bull is dismissed as a drink for Business majors, Floridians, and motocross enthusiasts. With so many crowning rectums, it is strictly in and out when it comes to the shared bathrooms, which in turn means that almost every tenant has their own bedroom mirror, to bask or wallow in as the case may be.

John Foreskin is in the main floor bathroom now, emptying his guts into the toilet bowl via his anus. He almost never gets up this early (before 10 AM). Nature's call was adamant though, and now, in his half-sleep haze, the birds chirping by the window are chirping *at* him, condemning the abomination now exiting his body and the lifestyle that precipitated it.

Why the fuck did I lug that bike all the way downstairs if I'm not even going to use it?

John's chronic issues in this department have led him to suspect a *third hole*, neither strictly rectal nor urethric, perhaps a vestige from the embryonic cloaca, perhaps hidden amongst folds of skin or else located further inside of the anus itself.

He abhors physical exertion. He really only enjoys walking, and then only if he's feeling himself à la mode de popped jean jacket collar and a good hair day, where good is defined as greasy yet voluminous like George Michael's hair circa *Wham!* Pushups are absolute hell for John's arrested heart chakra. All this means that he permits residence to a mirky nebula of abdominal humours, ones he could easily vanquish with a few yoga planks or a serious jog through nearby Pacific Spirit Park or the track at UBC. We see these humours in the dark circles under John's eyes and in his penchant for refined sugars. He alone sees them in his stool. John *was* an active child. His parents signed him up for soccer and summer camp and skiing. But his parents aren't the bosses anymore. Except for sending him money on his birthday and Christmas, they aren't anything. On rare occasions he cannot account for, he bears well-formed little dumplings or else power logs (a.k.a. battle spears) that exit without a trace, and he rises from the throne triumphant, sometimes even with a snippet of gratitude. But all the other times he is mocked by a sloppy mess that on some level he knows is his punishment; after which, hyper-conscious of his rectum, he skulks back to his basement sanctuary, and his mirror, where the sleights of vanity might once more find him in favour.

For all sluggards, there is hell to pay.

It feels true.

And from the Bible.

John Foreskin is relentless with his wiping this morning, which turns into plucking, then full-on excavation. But his asshole is like a hemophiliac's bayonet wound.

He risked takeout again last night, so he knows he has only himself to blame, for he long ago formulated the following:

> Premise 1: Delivery/takeout food (almost always) causes me horrible diarrhea, or at least unpleasantly sloppy shits.
>
> Premise 2: P1 is the case because either
>
> a. The cook hates his job and has inadvertently allowed his Nietzschean ressentiment to seep into the food.
> or
> b. The cook has a personal vendetta against me and has purposely imbued the food with all of his malice like Sauron did the One Ring of Power.
>
> Premise 3: I am unaware of having made any enemies who work in the food service industry.
>
> Premise 4: I remain, as a rule, aware of every enemy I make.
>
> Premise 5: [P1 + P2 + P3 +P4] All food service workers[6] hate their jobs.
> ~
> Conclusion: My diarrhea is principally caused by the disparities of wealth and dignity inherent in capitalism's dominance hierarchy.

---

[6] Backbone of the basement-dwelling, room-sharing Vancouverite underclass.

When it's finally over, John stands, entrapped by the bathroom mirror, sweating, bemoaning his hairline, and interrogating his life for the moral cause of its slow but undeniable recession. The shame of the exodus lingers like a sickly smog over his entire catholic area. As he checks his hairline from multiple angles, his thoughts stab backward to le Kyle's trans-ethnic challenge, then to Brad Pitt's hairline circa *Ocean's 11*.

He shivers as the creaking of a distant door finally breaks his reverie. Time for Starbucks. And a smoke. In the seconds it takes to reach his basement sanctuary, he has already made a solemn vow to use his exercise bike more and masturbate less—and then only out of biological necessity, never out of self-pity or to relive past glories.

Cool outside. Still not 10 AM. John stands on the front porch and lights a cigarette before checking his email. A reply from his mom, and she's attached two photos. He reads the poem:

Afternoon Tea

In a quarter most unruly
Sits a half-man bent and drooling
Fully given to the voices
In denial of his choices

Down a back way far from light
Sulks the exiled acolyte
Peeking out from closedrawn curtains
Paying dues to closeheld burdens

And up a path of gravel stone
Stalks a wayward all alone
Brow backed up with old accounts
Hating god with every ounce

And down the laneway off the path
Streaks a haggard bombadast
Preaching to her feline pretties
Laughing at your frightened pity

And in a rundown off the alley
Lives the girl who has no family
Says she lost them in a fire
Says she lives with no desire

And in a one-room by the bay
Stays the man whose nerves are frayed
Inviting one and all for tea
And he is I, and I am he

There's the line!

Brow backed up with old accounts.

The Basic Formula of the Patriarchy!

My formula!

He reads the poem one more time, cigarette dangling from his mouth.

I'm the wayward!

Wait—No. I'm the acolyte!

Somehow—somehow I'm all of them...

This has to be related to le Kyle's challenge...

The other photo's of the book cover. It's just as John remembers, leather-bound, with gold embossed writing:

The Collected Works
of
Prudence Moonweather

John sniffs his fingertips. Beneath the cigarette, he can smell the bathroom hand soap, and beneath that, last night's joint. He inserts them beneath his shaggy bangs to feel out the contours of his temples.

Brow backed up with old accounts...

Paying dues to closeheld burdens...

The man whose nerves are frayed...

But then...

When exactly did I become this way?

How did I lose track…?

Of my own cunning?

He looks at the poem again. Strange, medieval illustrations adorn the margins. A gremlin, or perhaps goblin. A witch. An old man leading a homunculus on a leash. And in the bottom left corner, a group of schoolchildren praying on their knees.

What the actual fuck?

He takes another drag of his Belmont. He can feel his morning yolk forming, and a slight breeze reassures him of distinct post-latte possibilities involving used bookstores, wooden park benches, and restful patches of shade. He looks up at the clear, blue sky.

Why haven't I been writing poetry these days?

I could.

I have before.

It could help me get to the bottom of things.

So what's stopping me?

I lost my old moleskin. That's what.

Some fuck probably stole it.

He checks his other emails.

Dear Mr. Foreskin,

We tried contacting you by telephone, and your mother provided me with your email address. As you may have heard, Dr. Reynolds retired back in 2011. She left all her patient medical records in our office. We are looking to get those into your hands if you are interested.

If you require them to be mailed to you, there is a $20 mailing fee, as this service is not covered by MSP. Alternatively, you or a family member (with your consent) is welcome to pick these up at no cost. Please let me know how you would like to proceed.

Thank you,

Tiyana

Dr. Yang's Office

107-3658 McCarthy Road

Ottawa, ON K1H 0B1

—

Hi Tiyana,

Thanks for contacting me. I would like to have the records mailed to me. What methods of payment do you accept?

J Foreskin

When John finally looks up from his phone, his first smoke of the day is almost finished. He snuffs it in the can by the door then jumps off the front porch and heads towards 10th Avenue.

Maybe the baristas will be different today.

Maybe they'll be guys.

He begins imagining how those interactions might proceed, given that he's wearing his slightly oversized, made-in-Sweden, red, canvas pullover hoodie, and his hair is greasy yet still voluminous.

10th Avenue is crowded. Young couples with children. Groups of students.

What day is it? Saturday?

John knows the girls that work the 10th and Tolmie Starbucks on Saturday mornings. He's already established his rapport with them, i.e. they're rather taken by his quirkiness and curious about what else he's capable of, including sexually. They'll notice his Swedish pullover without knowing that it's Swedish and without noticing that John notices them noticing. Even Corey commented on it yesterday in the park. John wasn't sure at first how he felt about it, that is, when he first discovered it at the Salvation Army on Broadway a few weeks ago. But after yesterday's adventure, he's sure he loves it.

He'll smoke one more cigarette, to prepare himself, then order his usual. This morning's shit has drained him quite a bit, and he doesn't want the sun to totally merk him before he even arrives at the café.

Nemesis.

The sun is Nemesis, Greek goddess of divine retribution.

Based on how he knows he looks though, plus the utterly gangster, quite-in-spite-of-his-credit-card-balance wad of cash he's carrying, literally anything can happen today. That's what being in his twenties is all about. He slows his pace to savour the cigarette.

As he nears the café, he makes out the unmistakable sheen of pomaded hair.

Seriously?

Does he just hop from one Starbucks to the next?

It's the man from yesterday. He's even got the same blue pamphlets. John scrutinizes his hairline. It's pretty much the best a high-born white man can hope for, where highborn is characterized by high blood sugar, milky-white skin, sharper features, and a distinct lack of soulfulness, where soulfulness is in turn defined as an attribute endogenous to BIPOC[7] individuals, and only ever appropriated by white colonialists and descendants thereof.[8]

"Nobody wants to be summarized," the man says with a sweeping gesture, "because everyone *thinks* they're complicated. Isn't that so?"

I wonder if le Kyle's ever seen this dude.

"Okay, but, perhaps you think you are simple?" The man all but sneers. "If I tell you what I really think of you, and it isn't flattering...if it doesn't *match* your self-image? Aha! You won't be happy, *will* you?"

John stops under the shade of a tree to finish his smoke.

---

[7] Black, indigenous, and people of colour

[8] Assuming the latter distinction is even meaningful

A couple, gaunt, thirty-something Rastafari Appro-priati,[9] have also stopped to listen, along with a petite professorial type with quirky frames who clasps her morning Starbucks like a prayer.

"How could anyone *possibly* understand you? Right? Does not each of us know much more about ourselves than about anyone else? Does anybody else even come close to knowing as much about you as *you* do? The countless moments you have experienced *as* you? Memories. Regrets. Secrets? *Sozen*, my friends, from our own point of view, the essence of who we are could never be captured by summary of stranger on street, yes? Of course," the man continues, clicking his mimed camera the audience, "we still make snap judgements of people all the time, yes? Snap. Snap." With this, the man pauses, garnering a few nods and a few frowns.

"Look at tree," he resumes suddenly.

The people to John, who can't really be touched thanks to his cigarette, fabulous hair day, and red can-vas pullover.

"Wizout complaining, yes? *Wizout complaining*, tree simply exists." The man turns almost mournful. "Wiz-out asking, it gives. It gives *so mach*." The man's voice

---

[9]Caucasian vegans with dreadlocks

cracks. The Rastafari Appropriati nod, mirroring his mood.

"It gives you shade to enjoy that cigarette," says the man, smiling at John.

John smiles back in spite of himself.

"It gives us clean air, and habitat for animals. All wizout self-conception. Not too complicated, yes?" The man flashes his crooked teeth. "And when it dies, when it dies it will give itself back to earth. With no self remaining. And when *you* die? What happens to whole life story after body has stopped working? After it rots? Does it die, too? But then, where do *you* go? What happens to all of that *me-ness* that you carry right now? Does your *soul* survive?"

An accusatory pause.

"No," the man says firmly, putting John on his heels. "Because humans have no soul."

John shares a startled smile with the professor.

"No *me-ness*. At least not in sense we usually conceive."

An older man makes to slip away.

"Please, sir, take a pamphlet. We offer free introductory seminars. Sunday. Come Sunday."

The man accepts the pamphlet with the slightest of bows, and the speaker turns back to the group. "But we make one for ourselves, don't we? A sense of self? By telling a story! Of who we are. Accomplishments. Victimhood. Enemies. And at the center? *Me,*" says the man with a shrug. "Always me."

"Indeed," says the professor, her eyes misty.

"But, but! Seelf we carry, wherever we go—that self we are aware of now, standing here, chatting—where does it actually exist?"

"In my mind," offers the male vegan, his voice much deeper than John expected.

"That is correct! *Only* in your mind. And what is the human mind?"

John sees his opening and ducks inside the café.

He's begun asking questions that he's already answered. He's trying to get us to go along with this account of things.

He starts thinking about what the man was saying, about self-conceptions, and where he might say *his* self actually resides.

The next thing he knows he's already ordered. He looks at the baristas, both girls. They seem content, possibly even amused.

What did I order?

Can they smell the cigarette?

He waits at the counter.

"You're not thinking of going, are you?"

"Well we'll see, won't we? That's what the free seminar is for." The man is holding a blue pamphlet.

"Oh Jesus, Frank. You know it's all hogwash."

"My free time is my free time, Linda. Lord knows you don't hear me complaining about your soirées."

"Those are for charity, Frank."

John claims an empty corner table with his hoody before heading to the bathrooms. Both are empty, and he chooses the one that feels cleaner. Sometimes the impulse to check his hair is irresistible. Like his brain is short-circuiting.

It looks fine though. Good, in fact. That's what the baristas saw. That's what the pomaded man outside saw. He massages his scalp with his fingernails and then ruffles his bangs. For show, he flushes the toilet and runs the tap.

"John? Your latte is ready."

John jumps out of his skin.

"They called for John. It was only drink left on the counter."

"Oh, thanks."

"Dudek," says the man, extending his hand. "A pleasure to meet you, John."

John shakes the man's hand. Not cold. Not warm.

"A pleasure to meet you, Dudek."

"I—"

"You were at the other Starbucks yesterday, near…"

"Dunbar. Yes."

"Did you..?"

"Did I what?"

"You left the pamphlet on my table."

"Yes," the man replies with a dignified air.

John finally sips his latte.

The man named Dudek smiles. "You look like a guy with a lot on his mind, John. Everything okay?"

"I'm fine," says John quickly. "I pretty much just woke up."

"I see. I see. John. Hence latte, yes?"

"Exactly." John smiles, then puts his hoody back on.

"Cold, yes? Starbucks is always cold."

"Kind of, yeah."

Dudek smiles as if waiting for John to say more.

"So…"

"So."

"So you're promoting some kind of…meditation?"

"Very good. Meditation."

John takes a long sip. When their eyes meet again, he finds himself returning the man's smile.

"We have a center. Here in Vancouver West."

"I see."

"You see. You see. Do you want to *see* the Center, John? I can take you. Right now." Palms upward, Dudek exaggerates a shrug.

"I mean…"

"What do you mean, John? Tell me!"

They both laugh.

"Sure? Alright."

"You don't have plans?"

"Not really, no."

"Good. Good. My car's around the corner. You follow me."

John looks out the passenger side window as they drive. He keeps losing himself in thought, forgetting entirely that Dudek is sitting right beside him.

It is almost as if…

He feels invisible.

Within ten minutes they turn onto a side street and park in front of a modest two-storey house.

"What street is this?"

"Balaclava," Dudek replies, making the name sound almost Italian. He turns off the car and then sighs deeply as he rubs his hands down his thighs.

The street is dead quiet.

John's mouth dries up.

What am I doing here?

"Are you ready to see Center, John?"

"Yeah. For sure." John yawns.

"Sleepy?"

"Yeah, somehow this latte isn't doing the trick."

"Yes. Coffee can do that," says Dudek, as if stating one of life's great maxims. "Don't worry. Hyemin makes *great* coffee. And feel free to smoke. In backyard." Dudek winks and then exits the car.

Hyemin?

Dudek sticks his head back in the car. "Shall ve?"

As John follows him to the front door, he nearly misses the small wooden sign on the lawn:

The Center

6

Finasteride & Alchemy

2022

"Granting a certain conception of time, as well as the familiar taxonomy of an otherwise arbitrary scale, there was once a planet…

And granting the sense of distance implied by this scale, we would say this planet was located in a galaxy rather far from our own.

And though the distance could be expressed mathematically, if we were being honest about our human mental capacities, we would say this galaxy was *unimaginably* far away.

And adopting a biological lens, we would be satisfied with saying that life dwelt on this planet.

Moreover, as it happened, one of the life forms dwelling on this planet happened to develop consciousness, and even self-consciousness, which is to say that one of the things they were aware of was *being aware*.

This lifeform understood itself to be living in time, much the way we humans do, experiencing it as moving forward linearly, if only because they were able to remember the past and imagine and plan for the future without being able to change the past and without knowing precisely what would happen 'next.'

Their planning and imagining abstracted their attention away from their present surroundings, as interpreted by their sensory apparatus.

As for this abstraction, it was commonly believed, as well as said, to *take place in* their heads (body parts which, if we were to gaze upon this lifeform, we would not hesitate to name as such). This may or may not have been a figure of speech, however, for among their top scientists and philosophers there was no consensus as to *where* all of their memories were stored, or *where* all of their imaginings took place. Different cultures and religions offered different accounts. Languages left clues about bygone paradigms.

Putting aside the present question, we may also wonder precisely *how* aware this lifeform tended to be. For they *were* conscious, and they tended towards being *self*-conscious, but they were not conscious of all their motives nor all their activities.

And by activities, we don't just mean inner operations of the organs and body systems that carry on without the conscious attention of the individual (as was the case for this lifeform), but operations of the will and the mind that manifest in outward action on the individual, familial, and cultural scales. Things like taking a selfie, goddamnit.

Of particular concern to us today is that this lifeform, who swam in the current of time, was not always aware of its own regard for the past.

But what could possibly be meant by this?

For one thing, if you were to tell a member of this species that they cherished their personal history, like a dragon guarding her gold, you would probably receive a reply that was in large part skepticism or even bafflement, but also, and in no small part, a kind of "so what?"—almost as if you had just stated a fact so obvious that nobody bothered to think about it. This is because, typically, this lifeform was not so much consciously as subconsciously engaged in the storing and preservation of its past, not so much consciously as subconsciously attached to all of—whatever it was precisely— they carried with them in—wherever it was precisely—they carried it.

What's more, this basic theme suffused their cultures, appearing in their traditions, their consumption, and their figures of speech. For instance, many of their consumer goods and services were marketed with phrases that might best translate as "create memories that will last a lifetime" or indeed "last forever." Other slogans spoke of particular moments in time as being "unforgettable," "precious," or "priceless" and of "capturing" them and never "letting go." Suffice it to say, the general project of amassing memories was almost, but not quite, universal among this lifeform.

And this 'not quite' is interesting, for it permits us to entertain a distinction that will divide the members of this species into two categories.

On the one hand, there were those members who believed, albeit subconsciously, that they were not, in fact, mortal, and who lived their lives accordingly. Consciously, they understood that their bodies would one day cease to function, whither, and then disappear, while subconsciously they did not believe that "they" —in the sense of the word *they* deemed important— would ever cease to exist.

Besides this group, a much smaller group had (by some whimsy of evolution or feat of will) become conscious of their belief in immortality. And among this second group, those who recognized this belief as either delusional or unjustified by and large worked to resist and shed it.

And we should say *worked* because the belief, being so deeply embedded in the collective subconscious of the lifeform, was by no means easy to shed, the motives and actions it spurred, by no means easy to resist and altogether cease.

Another distinction worth entertaining, which is perhaps already entailed by the belief in immortality, is between a member of this species and that member's body.

And it pertains as well to the question of *where* this lifeform is supposed to have stored their memories and imaginings, i.e. if not *in* the body and *in* the head, then where?

And of course, it pertains to the attitude this lifeform adopted towards those memories and imaginings, i.e. if these precious *things* did not die with the body, then perhaps it should indeed have been this lifeform's priority to seek out, 'make', and in many cases pay for "memories that last forever"—particularly so, we could further surmise, if whatever form they transitioned to after their bodies perished was unable to continue with the project of amassing memories, nor even, perhaps, of having now experiences.

In our own parlance, the above scenario would amount to something along the lines of curating one's own afterlife, while alive on the Earth, and therein dwelling for eternity after one's physical body has perished.

Now, among those who *had* become aware of this belief in immortality, certain individuals became obsessed with the possibility of *letting go*.

This obsession was motivated foremost by an acute somatic awareness of all they had accumulated over the course of their lives, all the *mind* (for that is what they chose to call it) that they could feel weighing them down, without, seemingly, being physically a part of them.

In tandem with the project of *letting go*, theories arose concerning the *why* of the accumulation, as well as the *how*.

It was not quite the same as eating, for that analogy crumbles when we consider that among members of this lifeform no known method existed for divesting oneself of the *mind* one had *eaten*. The analogy also falls short in so far as none among this lifeform supposed that the food they ate would remain theirs, inside of them forever.

It was rather the *experience* of eating that members of this lifeform almost universally sought out, motivated by the subconscious belief that to delight in eating something once was to capture that delight for eternity. It should not surprise you to hear that very often they did not consume food out of necessity but rather out of a desire to experience the satisfaction of eating—or indeed of *having eaten*—the satisfaction they remembered feeling, that they cherished, and that they wished to feel again.

This brings us to a very basic premise: members of this species, having once experienced something, and having stored that experience in their minds, were apt to develop *an appetite* for that experience.

Indeed, according to some of those concerned with *letting go*, it was understood that to have stored an experience of something in the mind (or the *heart*, as some preferred) meant precisely to have acquired an appetite for that something.

This would certainly go a long way toward explaining the spirit of epicureanism that pervaded their planet.

Nor were these appetites limited to experiences that we humans would consider to be pleasant. Indeed, we could distinguish entire subcultures, coteries, and covens devoted to seeking out experiences that we would consider off-putting, humiliating, and downright horrific. But it gets even better.

Because what if I told you that a considerable portion of this lifeform possessed abilities that we would call psychic?

And what if I told you that these psychics were no more likely to be aware of their abilities than of their belief in immortality (i.e. rarely and barely)?

Now I hope you are starting to get the picture of what I meant when I described this lifeform as being conscious, but not entirely. They were aware of what they were doing, and yet, they were not.

Please pause to consider the implications of this psychic aspect alongside the dynamic of appetites just now discussed.

What you may have already inferred is that those with psychic abilities were liable to develop appetites for the *felt experiences* of others.

And just as with the non-psychics of this lifeform, the flavour of experience hungered for varied from individual to individual, with psychics of a certain predilection often forming groups.

Examples: Some of these groups, akin to what we would call 'charities' included large numbers of psychic individuals with strong appetites for the *felt experience* of gratitude, meaning they fed off of *feeling others experience gratitude*.

Other members of these charities who possessed no psychic abilities whatsoever were simply preoccupied with satiating their appetite for the *lived experience* of pity, that is, feeling pity for others.

Conversely, a certain portion of the psychic population possessed an appetite for the *felt experience* of pity, i.e. pity felt by others *towards* them. You might say that these were the individuals most frequently targeted by the charities, but it would be more accurate to characterize the targeting as mutual.

You may not be surprised to learn that there were also psychic groups with a strong appetite for the *felt experience* of pain. You can easily imagine the kinds of activities these groups got up to, and we don't need to discuss all of them here.

A particularly interesting case emerges though when we consider the following intersection:

1. Individuals conscious of the belief in immortality.
2. Individuals with psychic abilities.
    2a. Individuals with an appetite for the *felt experience* of pain.

You may already be imagining some less than delightful outcomes of this confection, but the one I wish to mention might best be translated as: Vampire.

These were rare individuals who, conscious of their belief in immortality, chose to embrace it (rather than strive to shed it). Indeed, they used the belief to justify certain anti-social predilections that fed their appetite for the *felt experience* of pain. Put simply, they convinced themselves that consuming the blood of others prolonged their lives, even to the point of immortality.

According to a certain detached manner of thinking, however, these blood-suckers were no more perverse, no more deluded, than the various strands of hedonism, sadism, masochism, consumerism, and tourism, that proliferated across the planet taking their own parasitic tolls on surrounding individuals, populations, and ecosystems, all in the name of feeding an appetite, all in the name of storing up more."

John Foreskin awakes to a moaning erection of Orcish if not Macedonian connotation. He needs coffee. And nicotine. And not to look in the mirror. For his sleep has not been sound, which means that his forehead has no doubt grown overnight when time away from the demands of waking adult life should have shrunk it.

He accepts that, under the predominating paradigm, a causal link between cerebral activity and temple bulbousness is dubious at best. However, John has adopted a multi-paradigmatic approach to his hairline: the Pharmaceutical and the Alchemical.

He pursues the former via the daily oral administration of Finasteride, otherwise known as Propecia or Proscar. Finasteride was originally developed for men's

prostate health and was afterwards discovered to possess certain regenerative, counter-colonialist properties.

The alchemical aspect of John's regimen involves
solitary, meandering walks, meditation (earnest and
sweaty), plus the stern forswearing of refined sugars.
On no grounds he can articulate, he associates these
measures with the vanquishing of excess levity and the
subsequent loss of the faces now pushing back his hairline, faces saved by sniffing up past the brow.[10]

What he *could* tell you is that when he apologizes to
his FTLIJGF, sincerely apologizes, he does so *in spite of
himself*. At such moments, his voice lowers a full oc-
tave, often cracking, and there's an acute pricking in
his forehead as something up there is dislodged. And
that's when his eyes squeeze shut and his face contorts
until he loses all sense of how he might appear. And
that's when his heart finally opens and releases a pris-
oner. And that's when he loses a face.

John Foreskin readily accepts but rarely verbalizes
that his hairline obsession of twenty-plus years has
come to dominate every aspect of his life, both waking
and dreaming.

He has asked himself numerous times if he would
rather be completely bald and completely happy with
himself, or still have the hair he has but be completely

[10] See: The Basic Formula

miserable—or, if not *completely* miserable, then…the way that he is.

In answer to this question, he has never chosen happiness, not even secretly, because he cannot rule out the possibility that doing so would help to *manifest* baldness via the Law of Attraction.

John Foreskin steps out onto the balcony of his apartment heaven and exhales mango-passionfruit into a Universe that cannot be lied to. And he accepts his vanity. He knows no other way.

7
Working Diagnosis

2012

Why did I sign up if I'm not even sure if I'll go back?
Am I just a pushover?
Is it because of the Asian woman?

At the Center on Balaclava Street, a slender woman named Hyemin made John a delicious espresso from a real espresso machine. Then Dudek put some words and diagrams up on a whiteboard and explained how humans tell themselves a story about who they are and then live inside that story instead of living in the real world. He also talked about how to stop mental chatter, then something about finding and unravelling one's "root." John noticed how Dudek's accent thickened slightly whenever he went off whatever script he was obviously following.

Then John found himself paying $150 from his gangster's wad for one month's membership. Then Dudek made him stare at a small black circle taped to the wall for about twenty minutes until he got a headache. He called it a black hole and told John to throw all of his thoughts and memories into it while imagining that he had died and become a ghost. "Be-cause if have died, what is the point of holding onto all of it?"

Afterwards, he was famished, and Hyemin made him delicious fried rice that had peas, corn, carrots, and tiny cubes of pork. Throughout dinner, Dudek kept of-fering to drive him home, and John kept on insisting that he preferred to walk.

When it was finally time to leave, they gave him an-other pamphlet so that he could invite a friend to the Center.

It was almost as if…

It was almost as if they knew all of John's weakness-es. Hyemin's gaze bestowed both maternal approval and ethnic redemption, while Dudek's robust hairline sold John on the notion that this meditation could aid him on his quest to overcome le Kyle's trans-ethnic challenge. Between that and the food, John was practi-cally helpless. Plus, he didn't want to appear poor by *not* whipping out his fat wad of cash and paying for a membership on the spot.

But there was something else. Something spooky. Inside that house on Balaclava Street, John kept losing himself in thought, to the point where Dudek and Hyemin seemed to always have the jump on him, entering and exiting rooms without him noticing, and more than once, when breaking a silence, causing him to jump right out of his skin. John has always been able to feel people's presences. But Hyemin and Dudek didn't *feel* like anything at all.

That was over a week ago…

◈

John has walked a long way and now finds himself in a neighbourhood he doesn't recognize. He's not sure whether he has anything specific to do today, but it feels as if he doesn't, in addition to feeling like having too many specific plans can prevent one from simply going with the flow, following one's heart, discovering new parks, and stumbling across quaint cafés, used book stores, and thrift shops that nobody else knows about. Whereas, the whimsy produced by caffeine's upside is conducive to all of these things. Loose-fitting linen, too.

There's a party at Corey and Rick's tonight. Natural-ly, Rick will be there. Rick is part of East Van's mald-ing[11] back-lane gentry. He thinks faded black denim is a political statement and that it's better to have no bike at all than to have a bike that isn't a fixie. He works odd jobs and plays guitar. Not as well as Corey, but he's le-git at a few songs. He doesn't actually pay rent at Corey's. He lives just past Main Street, on the East side. But he frequently stays over in a way that is neither homosexual nor parasitic, and people just think of the house as "Corey and Rick's." Rick is already doing his MA in English or something like that at UBC. Segan might be at the party, too. Kerry definitely. Le Kyle. Everybody kind of knows everybody. It's mostly Arts undergraduates, or Arts graduates preying on arts un-dergraduates. Very incestuous.

The sun is behind some clouds and it's drizzling a bit now. John finds some park off a main road and sits down under a gazebo to smoke.

My whole life revolves around smokes now.

Whatever.

Some people are playing ultimate frisbee. They seem slightly older than John, working professional types in the early stages of onset adulthood.   John's not quite sure what side of King Edward he's on; he's never sure

---

[11] Mad and balding

where he is once he's a certain distance from the house. He could easily walk it to Corey and Rick's, but he decides to head home first for a quick shower because it's not even five o'clock and because who knows what could happen tonight.

On the way home he happens to pass a small used bookstore. He practically barges in, somehow out of breath, and notices right away that they sell moleskins. It feels like fate. He's back in business when the alchemical mood next strikes. The store feels like a well-kept secret, but John's red canvas hoody and shaggy hair announce that he belongs here.

The grey-haired shopkeeper watches him from beneath bushy eyebrows as he takes in the selection of Moleskins. He suddenly feels like a brand whore under the sway of consumerism, going straight for the least intellectual product in the store. He has half a mind to check the poetry section for a Prudence Moonweather volume, but he doesn't want to squander his momentum at the back of a musty shop only to come out with nothing. He settles on a red Moleskin, the hardcover kind, and pays from his wad. He exits the shop with the slightest of bows, making everything of the fact that he and the wizard-like shopkeeper exchanged exactly zero words.

The sun is back out, approving of John's current momentum. He puts the moleskin snuggly at the bottom of his knapsack and zips it shut, still in disbelief that he's never been to this neighbourhood before. Then, just a few doors down, he pops into a quaint café and ends up buying two Vegan Power Cookies and a 1L Perrier from a cute barista who can clearly tell what John is all about, both politically and philosophically. Paying from his wad of cash makes him feel like a potential provider in the eyes of the barista.

"Enjoy," she calls after him.

"Thank you," John says, spinning around. "Have a fantastic evening."

God, I love this hoody.

He almost goes back in to invite her to the party, but falters at the last second.

That would have been so chad.

When he arrives home, a large envelope is waiting for him on the hardwood floor of his basement sanctuary. It's the medical records from Ottawa.

He tears open the envelope to discover a manila folder that looks absolutely ancient. Among the papers are the records from every time John had to have a plantar wart removed from his left foot, plus two letters from his former therapist, Dr. Varma, typed on her office's letterhead and addressed to his family doctor.

He reads the letters:

September 13th, 2005
Dr. Reynolds
104-3328 McCarthy Road
Ottawa, Ontario
K1V0H9

Re: John Foreskin

Dear Shirley,

Thank you very much for referring this eighteen-year-old, gaunt university student, of Polish, Irish, German descent, catholic religious background, currently living at home with his sister and parents, who came in complaining of feeling anxious on and off for most of his life, especially during his teenage years, currently on no medication.

Patient's symptoms include frequent mood swings, feeling overwhelmed, restless, agitation, diminished concentration, despite which, he is able to maintain a B average at school; lack of motivation, impulsiveness, fear of growing bald, fear of being alone, fear of crowded places. He has panic attacks that last from minutes to hours. Each attack includes increased heart rate, shortness of breath, urgency to run, heaviness in the chest, sweating, and a lump in the throat. The frequency has been almost daily on and off for the past seven to ten years. There is also a deep body-absorption though no symptoms of anorexia or bulimia. There is also deper-sonalization. He does get auditory hallucinations, a very self-critical voice which is self-absorbed, though not sui-cidal or homicidal. He also gets visual hallucinations of blurry images around bodies and seeing shadows. He masturbates at least 10 times a day under a lot of shame. He is a self-proclaimed worrier about his looks and what others think. He has also developed a fair amount of avoidance behaviour where he avoids new people, parties, restaurants, and crowded places. He has developed all kinds of ways in which he has with-drawn. His hygiene is extremely poor. He stays up till 3:00 AM playing video games or, on weekends, usually out with friends, rarely ever sleeps by midnight and cannot remember the last time he had restful sleep. His current sources of stress are his sexuality and his confu-sion about his career path.

His family history includes he is the older of two chil-dren. He had difficulty coming up with adjectives for his parents. As a child, he described himself as being out-going, a people pleaser, and quite popular in elemen-tary school, yet when he went into middle school, he became an introvert, insecure, very nervous. His teenage years, he describes as extremely traumatic.

Currently, his emotional support is his girlfriend, though he describes his relationship with her as primari-ly sexual. Regarding exercise, he does some amount which is jogging. There is occasional alcohol. Drinks about one to two cups of coffee per day. He also smokes drugs on a regular basis, especially pot, up to two grams per day, no nicotine.

In conversation with him, I found him to be a rather scared, anxious, introverted young man with this glazed look in his eyes. He talked in a monotone. My working diagnosis with him currently is a panic disorder with agoraphobia, possibly secondary to substance use. I described to him the complete treatment program. At this time, he does not feel comfortable and decided he would speak to his parents about it and get back to me regarding what he wants to do. No future appointments were set up and he left on a positive note.

Axis I: Panic Disorder. Rule out psychosis secondary to substance dependence.

Axis II: Dependent personality traits & possible obsessive-compulsive disorder

Axis III: Deferred

Axis IV: Sexuality & Career

Axis V: GAF: 55

Thank you once again.

Yours sincerely,
Dr. Rupinder Varma, MD

John Foreskin is drenched with sweat. He Googles the axes:

Axis I: All psychological diagnostic categories, excluding personality disorder and mental retardation

Axis II: Mental retardation and personality disorders

Axis III: General medical condition; acute medical conditions and physical disorders

Axis IV: Psychosocial and environmental factors contributing to the disorder.

Axis V: Global Assessment of Functioning

GAF stands for "Global Assessment of Functioning," a scale from 0 to 100 with higher scores indicating higher levels of functioning.

The 91 – 100 range represents optimal mental health and coping capabilities.

Individuals with mild psychological issues fall in the 71 – 90 range.

But Dr. Varma gave me 55/100.

Was I really in such bad shape?

Am I now?

I know for a fact I've never masturbated more than twice in a single day.

So why did Dr. Varma say ten?

And why did she say I was German?

He tosses the papers onto the floor.

Maybe I do need meditation.

Maybe I need medication.

8

Feral & Athenian

2012

"You were very colicky as a baby. God, it was awful."

"Yes. Gaunt...Anxious."

Pre-party shower finished, John Foreskin stands naked in front of his full-length mirror. The papers from the doctor's office lay scattered on the floor.

Regarding himself from various angles, he wonders whether his current mould can be traced back to Dr. Varma's words, or even further back, to his mother's. Pressing closer to the mirror, he pushes back his wet bangs and examines the contours of his forehead. Is its prominence what affords him such a rich inner life? And is it the corollary of (what are surely) undiagnosed upper lung issues? Or, is he simply, in the classical Grecian paradigm, *malakas*—craven and effeminate?

Is that what Dr. Varma saw?

Is that what le Kyle sees?

Le Kyle once remarked during a shirts-optional backyard post-up session that they'd only ever seen one other man with "such a shallow chest." Then they looked John in the eyes and said, "He is a warrior, and that is the stamp of a warrior."

John takes a swig of his 1L Perrier, holding fast against the notion that le Kyle was patronizing him. More likely they were already grooming John for their trans-ethnic challenge.

Owing to his condition, burping is often so difficult that the gas from carbonated drinks ends up being expelled rectally rather than orally. And this is surely connected to the moisture marks he leaves on most seats. Plastic chairs bear a narrow streak of condensation. Pavement and stone surfaces are left dampened. Black fabric is best because it absorbs heat without a trace. Khakis and other light-coloured pants have simply not been an option since the start of high school.

KNOCK, KNOCK!

"John, are you home?"

Kerry.

John freezes, unsure of whether he's locked his door.

KNOCK, KNOCK!

"Hello?" she asks softly. "Hello, John. Are you there?"

She loves to say people's names. It's sweet really.

KNOCK, KNOCK!

She's nosy though.

"John? Aren't you home John?" she asks, as if not buying the silence.

John looks at his reflection in the mirror. He's not about to greet her with his hair this wet. He feels fifteen years older when it looks like this.

Finally, footsteps up the stairs. John listens, following them out the back door before sensing that he's finally alone. He closes his eyes to feel the entire house. It feels different when he's the only one at home. And that's what was scary, about the house on Balaclava. Even when Hyemin and Dudek were in the same room, he couldn't feel them.

He listens again. Nothing.

Different things become possible once he's alone. He throws on shorts and a t-shirt and bounds up to the main floor where he knows he'll find baby oil on the bathroom countertop and a can of beer in the fridge that nobody will miss. He makes it back in under a minute.

A half-hour later:

"Foals in winter coats, white girls of the north…"

A naked John Foreskin strikes various feral and Athen-
ian poses in front of his full-length mirror. *The Shins*
play softly from his laptop computer. He has shaved
the hair on his chest, belly, armpits, and Catholic area
down to the skin. He has applied generous amounts of
baby oil to every inch of his twenty-something male
Caucasian body.

"A latent power I'm known to hide…"

As he apprehends himself, a subtle weight begins to
lift. Waiting beneath the light-brown scraggles this entire time has been silky smooth glory. The one-word
barrier to his triumph stood for so long as "unnatural."
But this John Foreskin has finally rebutted with the following rationale:

Premise 1: Body hair and facial hair are not inherently different.

Premise 2: There is nothing "unnatural" about shaving facial hair.

Premise 3: I have been trimming my pubic hair for years without any negative consequences.

Premise 4: I am not subject to any cultural mores prohibiting the shaving of body hair.

Premise 5: Neither Google nor its subsidiary YouTube can confirm either of the following claims:

A. Shaving makes hair grow back with werewolfian vengeance.
B. The more body hair a man has, the more likely he is to go bald.

Premise 6: Even *if* manscaping does lend itself to homosexuality, I would at most become *bi*sexual, as my appetite for the inner thigh flesh of the female human, particularly that flesh not sullied by the sun, is insatiable.

∾

Conclusion: It is neither unnatural, nor taboo, nor hyper-pubescifying, nor crown-threatening, nor gay to shave one's body hair.

During puberty, the appearance of body hair stripped John Foreskin of his boyhood, and with it, his proximity to his mother. Yet these hairs have never been thick enough to be called truly manly, let alone Hasselhoffian. And now John Foreskin understands that these have been *optional* hairs. With time, they may yet grow into something chadifying. But he doesn't see that happening in his twenties, not like it has for his housemate, Yusef, or Rick for that matter.

John looks again in the mirror and belches out a combination of Perrier water and Kokanee beer. He feels close to truly losing himself in the Eminemian sense. He is refined. Sleekened. Oiled. Still Caucasian. But his tan from the summer hasn't totally faded.

Backyard post-up season. When it comes, they'll see.

It feels feminine to accept himself, and he imagines this is how women feel when they're "getting ready."

His time in front of the mirror has begun to drain him though. It *can* be an anti-mojo practice. John knows this. He takes one last look at himself, refusing to smile, then throws on the vagabond's perfect outfit, complete with his made-in-Sweden red canvas pullover hoody.

No sign of anyone on the main floor. He looks at the kitchen sink, full of dirty dishes again, slides over to the whiteboard, and snatches up the marker.

Whoever is leaving their dishes in the sink:
you keep doing it, I'm farting on your pillow!
(PANTS DOWN) = PINK EYE
FEAR THE STICK!

A few months ago things got really bad in the kitchen and a house meeting was called. Beers were passed around and each tenant was given a chance to speak their mind. It was somehow determined that the guys were mostly to blame, and after a few more beers they began threatening each other with fraternity-style humiliation if they didn't start cleaning up after themselves.

The new policy was inculcated with the refrain *"Fear the stick, fear the stick"* (referring to a particular wooden spoon that had become encrusted with chilli). But the chant ended up arousing more feelings of brotherhood and bi-curiosity than terror or homophobia. To John Foreskin's knowledge, none of his male housemates are sodomites. But on the night of the house meeting, at the frenzied crescendo of their drunken chanting, *"Fear the stick, fear the stick,"* les boys of 4474 West 14th unanimously gleaned the hypothetical necessity of such a union between man and man, and why Darwinian Nature, if not Abrahamic Heaven, might condone it.

John's got a nice buzz going from the beer now. Plus, his mirror session has necessitated a smoke, which he knows he ought to have on the back porch where the sun can hold him to account. He could even stroke back his bangs to give her a crack at his temples. He steps out and looks up at the sky.

Hello, my Nemesis.

The first drag is pure majesty, and he is once again filled with silent knowing. Self-pity, now, feels far away and foolish, and the birds chirping from the giant oak appreciate John for being at one with nature and the living Universe. Even the sun, halfway behind a cloud, seems only to approve of him and the levelling up that has just taken place in his room.

It doesn't help his nerves though that smoking remains a secretive business, a business that sees him gazing slit-eyed at every passerby in the laneway, a business that harkens always back to his father.

John takes another drag, no longer seeing anything in front of him, and, as he fondles his smooth, freshly oiled belly, his mind drifts to Ottawa and his childhood home on Uplands Drive…

Everything is what it seems at that young age when the voices of thought are not yet loud enough to be mistaken for oneself.

It is one of those summer nights when it feels like the sun is never going to set. Half the neighbours are out on their front steps, or in their backyards barbecuing, and the Dickie Dee ice cream guy has just done his evening ride-through, jingling his bells and inciting all kinds of squirmy commotion.

"John, time to come in!"

It feels unfair that he has to go inside before dark when so many other kids are still playing, and with so many possible victories remaining. But his mom has called him more than once, and she knows he's heard. So Little John Foreskin begins the inevitable walk home.

The crotch-high cement car plugins stand sentry, one for every two units, all around the courtyard. On dark winter mornings, they are life support machines that have kept all of the car engines from freezing overnight. During the endless days of summer, they are the lean-ons of discursive parents and the rub-againsts of children still small enough to get away with humping anything that doesn't object. And all the cars sit parked around the courtyard, one in front of each unit, telling Little John more or less who is home when he wants to call on somebody, or which backyards are probably safe to sneak into if a ball has strayed over a fence.

As he rounds the sidewalk home, he spots Mario and Ola vying with the passion in the pits of their stomachs. Something about Ola's dad and them being right on her front step makes it impossible for them to do anything about it. What they are left with (the spoken word) does so little to alleviate their adolescent affliction that they welcome the chance to greet John. Little John Foreskin pities them, not understanding, never guessing how, in just a few years, he will.

He enters unit 81, latching the screen door quietly and kicking his shoes off into the mayhem of the front hall. Walking into the living room, he plops down on the cool red and tan of the futon and toes off his socks. In the quiet of the evening, he can feel the entire house.

His eyes pick out the glass sliding door; a summer night, and it's only open a crack. Again, he feels the house. Silence. An air of secrecy wafts in through the crack then, along with a certain something else that any child could detect: the weight of adult self-possession.

John rises slowly, already certain of what he's going to find.

There, standing by the back fence, is John Sr., looking down the row of crabapple trees to the pink sky above the field where they walk the dog. John feels what his father feels: the quiet solace of the damp, dark greens, the seclusion created by the row of trees. It has always been a restful place, and John can feel its mood invite him whenever he walks around the side of their end unit.

"Yeah but, see, that's what I don't understand. It's like, do it right the first time, you know?"

People can always catch John Sr. speaking to himself, head abuzz, acting out hypothetical dialogues, going over the day's interactions.

Again Little John feels pity, again never guessing how well he'll one day understand. He slides open the heavy glass door. John Sr. snuffs out his cigarette on the parapet of the fence before recovering with his standard greeting.

"Hey, Bud."

"Hey."

Little John regards his father with the same skepticism he pays every adult male, but if John Sr feels it, it doesn't show.

Lingering now in the air is John Sr's guilty wish that his son hadn't interrupted his smoke and John Jr's conviction that he's been somehow victorious over his father.

In a few more years, when John Jr has even more of his own to nurse and protect, he'll begin seeking out that same seclusion, along with the guilty pleasures that take the edge off of the here and now. But on this

evening, sliding open the door and confronting his father came automatically and felt just.

A car engine revs, and John Foreskin finds himself
alone again, scanning the back lane of West 14th. As he
smokes his cigarette, head abuzz, that same feeling of
guilty sneakiness visits him so that, as a physically
grown man, he cannot help but look around to see who
might catch him in the act.

"So you *are* home."

John jumps out of his skin before recognizing the
voice and fianchettoing his malice into a tight-lipped
smile. He turns to look through the back door.

From the darkness of the kitchen, Dmitry's eyes
shine. *We live in a civilized society*, they seem to say.
What are you going to do, hit me?

"What's up, Dmitry?" John snuffs out his smoke and
steps back into the kitchen.

"Oh, you know, nothing much, " Dmitry says, slicking back his hair. "*You* seem relaxed though. I love your
hoody, by the way."

John looks away, furious at how much he enjoys the
compliment. Dmitry is what John calls ethnic-white.
Not Canadian. Not American. Something more exotic,
with a legitimate claim on capital-C Culture. His room
is on one of the upper floors, possibly the one closest to

le Kyle's loft, and more than once he's seen them walking down the stairs together. John hates Dmitry for being new to the house but already more social than he is, for knowing le Kyle way longer, and for always stroking back his hair.

"I brewed some of Kerry's dark roast. You want some?"

"Nah, I'm good. Of coffee these days."

Liar.

"Shitty shits these days, brother?"

Brother!

"I love the whiteboard message, by the way. I'm guessing that was you. People are slacking these days. They need to start fearing the stick again."

John opens the fridge.

"Take one of my Kokanees if you like. I'm doing a beer run before the party."

"What?"

"Yeah. People are saying the party is going to be here tonight," says Dmitry. "I mean, instead."

"Wait. Which party are you talking about?"

"The Party at Rick's? I just assumed you were going since you and Corey are tight."

"Rick's? You mean Corey's? How do you know about the party?"

"Bro, I'm taking Lit-Anal with Rick. At UBC? I asumed you knew that."

"Right." John is suddenly sweating as if he didn't just smoke that jizz-tier cigarette out back. He rubs his belly, the smoothness still novel, and is grateful when another Kokanee burb escapes his chest.

Dmitry's Kokanee.

"By the way, le Kyle and I have been playing more chess lately," says Dmitry, slicking back his hair. "You should get in on it. Kerry gave us pointers last time."

John wants to sit and rest his nicotated legs. But sitting feels like yielding. He finds himself envying how coarse and straight Dmitry's hair is, if only because his own is so fine and frizzy.

"Bro?"

"What?"

"I asked if you're coming to the party."

"You told me you were an engineer and that you worked downtown."

"So?"

"So why are you going to UBC then?"

Am I drunk?

Dmitry looks flustered. "I'm doing a part-time M.A. I'm allowed to like literature, am I not?" He sucks his teeth. "Why are you interrogating me?" And then, half to himself: "You're worse than le Kyle."

"What?"

"Nothing. Forget it. I just don't get your question."

"My bad. It's been a fucked up day. I got a package from—"

Dmitry's phone starts buzzing up the counter.

"I have to take this. Excuse me." He passes out the back door with his phone and mug of coffee.

John sits down in the living room and stares at the blank TV screen.

Was I actually about to tell him about Dr. Varma's letter?

Is that what I do? Spill my guts after being an asshole?

And what did he mean, worse than le Kyle?

He looks out the window, wondering why Corey hasn't texted him yet if the party's actually moved.

And how the fuck does Dmitry find time to do an MA?

Or the money.

He jumps up from the couch and heads out the front door. Only aimless momentum can save him now from articulating in human language that Dmitry has his shit together way more than he does, that he's intelligent, deserving of love, not evil, and very likely tighter with le Kyle than he'll ever be.

9

The Party:
Part I

2012

The party will be held at John's house after all (something about Corey's landlord ordering a plumber for the next morning). Enough people from both houses know each other anyway.

John Foreskin doesn't care. His room has a lock. That's always the main thing with parties—somebody getting drunk and then potentially pissing in one of your drawers or on your bed, or puking there, or doing it sober just because they think they can get away with it because they hate you.

Now John just needs an in-between to work off his encounter with Dmitry and so that he can arrive later than most people, and with vigour from having exerted himself. He's wearing the same red Swedish pullover he's been wearing for days now, allowing his natural musk to fortify his pre-party mood. He's not sure what street he's on, but there should be a park up ahead that he vaguely remembers smoking at with Corey and Rick one time, one where he can reflect in solitude yet still be gazed upon by women in their thirties who already have careers and dogs and hatchbacks with ski racks, women who may be able to tell that something is different about him tonight without guessing that it involves his body hair. He's chosen only nicotine for the excursion.

Hours later. Finally late enough to feel legit. And John has cultivated a certain sternness that he can feel pushing his forehead downward into what he hopes resembles the vertical action-star furrow.

The walk back to West 14th is vigorous with plenty of reassuring eye contact plus several distinct victories over people who underestimate how activated John's mojo is. It is walks like these when he feels at once like a good boy and a young man of brimming potential. The only other time when these two facets of himself synchronize is when he ejaculates inside of a female. At the height of his conquest, he feels more powerful than Brad Pitt circa *Troy*. But the very next moment, *she* is the one cuddling *him*, hushing out his convulsive sobs, and reassuring him, when prompted, that he is indeed a good boy.

The house is alive when John arrives. Noble millennial savages subsisting without a thought for tomorrow, let alone retirement.

John slows his pace slightly as if to say, *"Yes, I live here, in this happening house, but no, I am not particularly interested in what is currently taking place."* He still finds himself guesstimating the males who may have shown up though, including Dmitry, and which ones might have the power to shame him with a "buddy" greeting or a too-firm pat on the back, even now that his mojo is in full gear.

Since you were about to ask, within the walls of 4474 West 14th, toxic masculinity manifests in various ways, including but not limited to:

- sideburns
- drinking beer
- the affirmation "good tuneage" evoked by music
- possessing knowledge
- rough & tumble play
- accomplishing tasks
- televised athleticism evoking emotions everyday conversation can never come close to touching
- stern agreement

- ejaculating into a toilet bowl (solemnity optional) after having forgone masturbation for at least seven consecutive days
- getting the last word in
- reticence to the point of masochism
- facial hair
- Secretly having sexual thoughts about women
- striving to defeat others in sanctioned competition
- body hair
- addressing other males as "buddy"
- wanting badly to win
- taking stairs two at a time
- pumping it hard with a consenting partner
- pumping it hard in a workout
- burping

The party is in full swing when John enters. He can smell people agreeing about things and fending off silences with aggressive, throaty observations about life. These are typically normative or descriptive statements that carry the charismatic implications of a question, in so far as the listener always feels pressured to respond and thereby raise the collective brow that much higher.

The tension excites him. He knows that at least 25% of them will be having sex by the end of the night, and that at least 50% of that sex will be regretted by at least

50% of the parties involved. He feels strategically detached from all of it.

The interior of the house is in its usual shambles. All of the tenants originally signed up for a lifestyle that protests Adulthood and, more concretely, the oppressive White Cis Hetero Post-Colonial Patriarchy. Their lifestyle precludes majoring in business as well as feeling any gratitude for parents or the paved, colonized portions of the world said parents have brought them into. This makes contributing to any of the common areas of the house rather difficult, to say nothing of the world at large. John's is an age group who remain subconsciously skeptical that "the future" will ever actually arrive, and who pass every night accordingly.[12] The morning always comes, but never to disprove their theory, and so student house showers go years without proper cleaning and credit card balances months without checking. Planning for the future is what parents with RRSPs do, and parents live sedated, divorced lives.

John wades through the crowded hallway towards the kitchen. He overhears a mansplainer misuse the term "essentially" but refrains from correcting him. The hooka crowd will be in the living room, with their chill intolerance of anyone who appears too hype to possi-

---

[12] See: Mayan Calendar

bly be keeping it real, and he's sure that Dmitry will be among them. Somebody in the living room asks "What's the vibe?" and John shudders to think how white they likely are.

A mousey girl wearing big headphones slips by him with a glass of something pink and a bag of pita bread. John knows her for her taciturn face, her freckly, milky-white skin, and for requesting hummus whenever Mark the Theatre Major makes Costco runs. Mark drives and has his shit together more so than most guys John knows who aren't engineering students, and/or East Asian with tiger moms. Sometimes HUMMUS is written in all caps on the kitchen whiteboard on the day of a run. Besides requesting and retrieving hummus, Mousey Girl barely leaves her room or speaks to anyone. John has put her in the category of girls he possibly stands a chance with. To make inroads with any of the alpha females like Kerry, he would have to affect a chadness that he feels is not really in him; plus he would have to know about craft beers, be eager to take his shirt off at the beach, and probably also drive a car that has a ski or bike rack. John knows this has to do with him being less guy's-guy material than le Kyle, Corey, Rick, Yusef and most cisgender, pack-mentality bros. Mousey Girl disappears up the stairs before John can make any kind of gesture.

The kitchen is brighter, and just as crowded as the hallway. The counter is littered with red party cups and all kinds of sex potions promising to vanquish inhibitions as well as a number of behaviours associated with high-functioning autism.[13] Somebody did the dishes while John was out and his whiteboard message is gone. He immediately downs two shots of rum, hyperconscious of his audience. Then he tucks in his tailbone to correct his posture. Then he mixes two other random drinks and finally adds iced tea, uncertain of how the sugar and caffeine content will affect his mojo.

A gust of fresh air comes in through the back door and suddenly he's never been happier to be in his twenties. He stands on one leg, in a pose that makes him feel solid, then finally dares a look into the living room.

The hooka crowd is about six strong including two Rastafari Appropriati who John recognizes from a park sesh during the Summer. No Dmitry though. Corey is playing his guitar on a beanbag. He cocks his head to offer John the spliff in his mouth.

"Later!" John shouts above the music, and Corey points at him, as if to make it a pact.

Kerry's in the living room, too, wearing tights plus some kid-size t-shirt on top that says 'popcorn' in bub-

[13] More or less an epidemic among millennial Arts majors

ble letters. She's enslaved a few business major types who sit around her fawning and thinking they stand a chance. John catches her eye and wants to motion for a smoke. It would be pretty chad if she were down.

Don't be desperate.

He raises his cup instead and offers a smile. Kerry's look is this maternal *good for you* that at once affirms everything between them. John Foreskin's heart chakra blooms. If Kerry weren't so tall and powerful and confident and articulate, John might stand a chance with her. It would practically be incest though, in so far as Kerry is Caucasian and so are John's mother and sister, not to mention John. They probably both grew up eating potatoes, salmon, Caesar salads, and watching cartoons like Doug and Hey Arnold before getting precociously into Seinfeld and, later, Project Runway.

Super incestuous.

He considers the backyard then, but it sounds so lit and populated by males that he knows better than to attempt an entrance. He turns back through the kitchen and then makes his way down the hall with just a little more bounce in his step, plus the hankering for a smoke that at least provides a clear purpose.

Pushing his way through the crowd, he grazes breasts, hairy forearms, and sweaty backs. But the breasts feel matter-of-fact, not hentai, and the sweat makes him love humanity instead of hating it.

Somebody gives his shoulder a squeeze and John knows without looking that they care about him and wish him the best, precisely the way a Buddhist recognizes every sentient being as seeking to escape the cycle of samsara. He sashays between the bannister and a girl he doesn't know by placing the tips of his fingers on the small of her back. He feels powerful and alive and in love with all of them.

The front porch is pretty lit as well, but more discursive—Humanities majors engaged in the white privilege of scholé, most likely. John hopes that nobody remembers seeing him come in. He finds a seat lower down the steps and lights a cigarette, nodding to a few people in the middle of conversations. A Boomer couple is walking by on the opposite sidewalk. Their dog looks sad, and John intuits the cause to be the couple's unliberated sex life. He pities them as he pities all adults.

No sign of le Kyle yet.

Maybe they're out back.

I think I'm finally getting used to his pronouns.

Their pronouns. Fuck!

John wonders how the past few days have affected his hairline and whether he'll be able to recultivate the mood from after his park session with Corey.

"Sometime before the genesis of dipping sauces, pizza *was* good enough on its own. That's all I'm contending."

"He's not wrong."

"But now. *Now*, when presented with the choice, when offered a reasonably priced garlic dipping sauce, few people can turn it down."

"Few people? I think you're over-esteeming the dipping sauce, my friend."

"Is he though?"

"Jesus Christ, Yusef. You're like a gnat buzzing in my ear."

"I mean, that's funny," Yusef retorts, in a raspy, accented voice, "because, because of course the irony of mosquitos is that they come and annoy the hell out of you, but in fact—and I've verified this empirically— if one relaxes one's body completely, the vibrations one then emanates actually *repel* the mosquitoes. It's like, it's like they're not there to *cause* annoyance per se; they're there to *feed* off of it."

"There you have it folks."

John does his best to ignore the surrounding conversations, knowing they'll only distract him from le Kyle's trans-ethnic challenge.

He can feel the nicotine from his cigarette opening a porthole into the alchemical paradigm. He straightens his spine and presses the balls of his feet into the wooden porch step.

After a few more drags, a viscous backlog of humours begins to seep through his brow and down his Polish nose, making his upper lip quiver and ache with release.

Unaired grievances.

The thought comes out of nowhere, and John does not question it. It only confirms the Basic Formula:

- To let pride down past the brow feels like losing
while
- To retain things there and accumulate even more feels like winning

Brow backed up with old accounts.

Learned from my father. Who learned from his father before him, and so on, back to the first patriarch.

Some of it's coming undone now!

Is this what Dudek meant when he spoke of finding my root?

The humours continue to seep downward, thick like tree sap. John can feel his upper lip curl to reveal his canines. Having hardly ever expressed open wrath, he's sure that he appears to the others as some kind of grotesque gargoyle. He barely resists the urge to intervene, to save face. To any onlooker though, he now appears only mildly perturbed.

His eyes begin to well up and shine as he gives himself over to the process. He knows that beyond his blurred vision, the people around him are perfect and beautiful. And he's reassured that they want to approach him and talk but are also deeply intimidated, as one would have been by Siddhartha Gautama sitting under his bodhi tree.

As the catharsis subsides, John's head begins to ache the way it did at the Center after he'd focused on the black hole for twenty minutes. His body feels lighter, but tired. He lets out a deep, acidic burp and then finally permits himself to look around.

10

Bedtime

1993

Taxonomy of a seven-year-old's lived experience:

- Secrets: Reside within, known only to oneself.
- Reputation: Resides within, known to oneself and others.
- Facts: Things not to forget.
- Pride: What one holds onto. Possibly Secret. Articulated in mentation as Facts, and/or sensed somatically as inertia.
- The Universe: The one that knows all and reclaims all. The one that is always there.
- Love: A living energy. To be found boundless within, or else sought from others.

At bedtime there is weeping and gnashing of teeth.

Nobody desired is spared.

Nobody ravenous denied their share.

The affections of the mother are preferred over those of the father.

Secrets are kept.

Bonds consolidated.

Facts checked.

The masculine shunned.

It is dark when the lights are off in the bedroom.

The light in the hallway stays on till the parents go to bed.

They need alone time.

Downstairs.

The son and daughter are to respect that.

TV and conversation.

At bedtime, the son is all tucked in and waiting.

Tense from everything he's claimed and committed to.

Tense against God.

Not the catholic god from his school prayers.

The Universe.

All three want the mother's affections. But the father's desires are different. He'll have her to himself after the son and daughter have been put to bed. They need to get as much as they can first. But neither child wants to be tucked in first. It is better to have her second and get all that remains before the alone time.

The son is determined to keep her with him as long as possible. For she is the great wellspring.

The son has already made the choice to hold on to his Original Secret and so to be a lesser wellspring.

The father is more craven than the son. The son doesn't want that for his mother. So each night he asks her to stay and sleep in his bed. They could sleep together the entire night, and the father would be left alone, to know that the son has become the one. But she always says no.

The son knows he is his mother's son and that he is handsome. These are two of the founding facts of life, the former anteceding even his name and the incident precipitating the Original Secret. Handsomeness is the primary fact of his reputation and the highest point of pride that isn't also a secret.

And the son knows that he is a good boy. This is not a secret, for teachers speak of it, as do both grandmothers, as does his mother to him in front of others. So not a secret, but yes a fact, born of the private moments between the son and the mother, and there again each night reaffirmed.

The darkness conspires with sleep to erase the facts from the son's mind. The son's main objective is to reaffirm them. This might precede the mother's entering as he waits for his sister to have her turn, and it always succeeds it, as he is never sleepy once she's left.

The son listens through the wall and knows that the tuck-ins the mother shares with him are different from those she shares with the daughter.

The son's tuck-ins aren't secret, but their proceedings are. In the darkness, his other senses come alive, and when they cuddle, he stops knowing where his body ends and hers begins. The fact of being her son is here reaffirmed through words and touch. That he is a good boy is asked and answered, for if it were not, the Universe would eventually reclaim it, and it would cease to be a fact.

Before the mother leaves, the son elicits the fact of his handsomeness. This he does by telling her that she is beautiful. Her response is to beam while squeezing him into herself even more deeply. And in the darkness where empathy reigns, the son beams as well, mirroring the pride he's ignited in her and storing it with the lump sum that gives him strength enough to endure the times when they are separated. Finally, she speaks the words he needs to hear. And the son exalts.

The facts having been upheld, the son is primed for the alchemy he must complete before sleep overtakes him. He will wake in the morning still knowing what is true.

It has always been this way, for forging himself: a fight against the darkness that would swallow him up, by making him forget.

For if he forgets himself, the Original Secret might escape. It holds fast in his lower back, on the left side, extending its roots down to the tips of his left toes and upwards into his heart and right eye. He stows it away when she comes in to love him. But when she leaves, he relents. And again it flexes. And the closet door creaks and the window pane raps as the space around him stretches to accommodate it.

Then the son lies awake completing his alchemy until long after the others have fallen asleep, long after the affair between the mother and the father. With only the hallway between them, the son feels all of it. The dark hunger that pursues her, that she welcomes. The deep lull that follows. And finally, sleep. He never permits himself to sleep until it is over with.

11

The Party: Part II

2012

John Foreskin turns around, baby-eyed from his cathar sis. The front porch is a who's who of the Vancouver West millennial scene.

"Yo Foreskin," says Basement Yusef, "you get the envelope I slipped under your door?"

John nods. The envelope. Dr. Varma's letter. The Center. Le Kyle's trans-ethnic challenge. It's like his whole life has been leading up to this moment.

He looks again at Yusef sitting at the top of stairs looking like a 1920s wrestler in his wife-beater, his thick black hair restrained to military dimensions. John finds this absurd since it would be glorious (ethnically) if he grew it out. Basement Yusef was the one behind the wooden spoon policy: *"Fear the stick, fear the stick!"*

117

He's one of the only housemates who never drinks coffee, preferring tea with milk and sometimes a cube of white sugar. His continence is so apparent that John knew him at first glance to be a once-in-two-days pooper, possibly three.

John catches himself looking at Yusef's hairline. More than once, he's marvelled at how well Yusef seems to understand his own temper, never allowing it to fire up and sear his mane, knowing always how to placate it with nicotine, fatty acids, and frequent small sips of his tea.

John knows better than to seek confirmation that Yusef's hair is more black than it is white. Whether Arab is a distinct race, he hasn't yet decided, nor is it the kind of inquiry one trusts to Google or its subsidiary, YouTube. Somehow or other though, Yusef shares something with le Kyle that John feels is off-limits to him, Kerry, and other white people.

Call it flavour
Call it juice
Walk a mile
In the black man's boots.

For every unspoken truth, a song bears witness and testifies, even if John's upper right temple has to make it up all by itself.

Beside Yusef, the East African nubile, christened Segan Abraham, is sprawled across three levels of steps. Segan's a Biology major who models part-time and has some classes with Kerry. Her first name means ostrich and apparently ordained the ungodly length her legs would grow to. Her prominent eyeballs are the focal points of a face so avant-garde in its beauty that Caucasian men brainwashed by Baywatch and Victoria's various pencil-thin Secrets too often mistake it for unpretty. John Foreskin understands this despite having recovered from his adolescent bout with Jungle Fever.

Like Yusef, Segan is fully aware of the currency her ethnicity carries in Vancouverite-millennial circles (to say nothing of academic administrative offices), but her essential ethnic strength—made apparent to John by the nappiness of her hair (and retained despite her post-colonial surroundings and the human propensity to imitate)—is that she does not indulge in masturbatory amounts of brow-raising, which is to say nothing more than that Segan always keeps it real.

Her tolerance of the entire Vancouver West millennial scene is a grand gesture of condescension that no white person except John Foreskin has put a finger on.

Segan nods, and John nods back. He wonders if his face looks any different from a moment ago when he stepped outside. But it seems as if even Segan has no idea of what's just happened to him.

Heads turn to the curb as the hefty but composed Siyavash emerges from his hatchback Honda.

As a rule, Siyavash avoids any eye contact or conversation topic that might set off his temper. His whole mystique in the house swirls around the fact that nobody has seen that temper directed against a member of the house or anybody else in Canada. He only loses it when talking long distance with his mother or fiancé in Pakistan. These eruptions are heard by housemates through closed doors and from floors away, either when Siyavash takes his meals alone in his room or when he's sitting on the toilet. He rushes neither activity, and John has inferred a causal link between this trait and Siyavash's quite-in-spite-of-his-temperament hairline.

"Salam alaykum," Segan calls out.

Siyavash manages a weary wave. "Wa alaykum assalam."

Siyavash rents a room on one of the upper floors, which means he uses the same toilet and shower as the Mousey Girl. And if that isn't pornographic, then John Foreskin doesn't know what is. Siyavash studies engineering at UBC[14] and holds down two different gas station jobs. He cooks his own meals and doesn't smoke weed. He only drinks to celebrate the end of exams, and, as a rule, he doesn't mix sugary drinks with his alcohol.

John has often speculated on the adjacency of Arabs to Pakistanis, but the tenuous rapport between Basement Yusef and Siyavash has yielded precious few clues.

Kerry once hypothesized that Siyavash has a rice cooker in his room and that he uses the upper-floor bathroom as a source of cooking water. He is practically never seen in the main-floor kitchen, and he has never once partaken in the "tear the stick" rituals.

Siyavash begins his approach, seemingly unfazed by the waves of privilege emanating from the predominately Caucasian party. After a brief mental scramble, John assumes the airs acquired from fraternizing with le Kyle, drawing heavily from his reservoirs of street cred and down-to-earthness. But Siyavash is looking past him, to black-denim-clad Rick who has appeared from the side of the house and who now offers Siyavash a cigarette.

"Rolled it myself, bro. Fuck pre-fabs."

---

[14] i.e. Like, Dmitry, he has a more or less square-shaped head.

Fucking Johnny on the spot.

Rick must have been part of the backyard brouhaha that John chose to avoid.

And now he's brought that gusto with him to farm the front porch.

Siyavash accepts the cigarette and, in a moment of fragile chadhood, even allows Rick to light it. They squint at each other during the first inhale before proceeding to grind out a perfectly masculine dialectic.

The general areas covered are health, politics, money, school, gaming, and women, with the topic changing each time one of them determines this to be his only way of saving face. Any utterance by one is met with an utterance by the other, a fundamental law that makes parting ways rather difficult. They find much in common though. Neither can remember having ever yielded—in any sense of the word—to any human being—ever. They both consider sexual intercourse to be the highest form of victory, while neither considers masturbation as necessarily a defeat.

Besides agreeing or disagreeing—two states of affairs acknowledged by each—each either knows, or doesn't know, what the other is talking about. When ignorant, the listening bro either finds some angle of critical analysis, or else changes the subject, or else replies with a simple *"interesting."* Both bros take for granted that knowledge is indeed power, yet shun overt curiosity because, while it can remedy ignorance, it also betrays it.

"Something something intersectionality, something something Venezuela," Ray offers. "Wealth distribution something something."

Siyavash raises an eyebrow. "I send half my wages back to my family, in Pakistan. I just hope I can keep my scholarship next term."

"Something something about never skipping leg day."

"Something something whey protein powder post-workout."

"Granted, but something about one's kidneys. Not to mention something something the retention of semen during intermittent fasting."

"Something something Ramadan was in July this year..."

"Hmm. Interesting."

Neither bro yields. Neither submits. Their conversation has served to affirm the eternal male-on-male tension, to momentarily awaken it, but not to resolve even a single iota.

John supposes that if coaxed via CIA torture and/or CIA LSD to say what each seeks from the other, both bros would vacillate between killing his counterpart and straddling him sexually—or both in the reverse order. There is always so much unresolved tension between grown men and precious few ways to get to the bottom of it without breaching either the hetero orthodoxy or the laws of civilized society.

John rises to make his exit, garnering silent nods from multiple genders and ethnicities on his way to the front door.

Back inside the house, there's a lot of pensive nodding to dope beats. John heads to the kitchen to hydrate and mix himself another drink. A guy and a girl are making out in the hallway. Both Caucasian.

Disgusting.

The guy is darkly tanned like a farm boy from Alberta or Brad Pitt circa *A River Runs Through It*. The girl's neotenous features and spunk tell John she's still in first year and hasn't yet ruined herself with drinking and sex like most of the crow-throated third- and fourth-year white girls who, quite apart from connotations of incest, have utterly ruined Caucasians for John. He observes the couple for slightly too long before moving on.

After preparing himself a rum and coke, he enters the living room fully agreeing with Sartre that *hell is other people* yet also certain that he can withstand the aggregate gaze of the oh-so-chilled-out hooka crew. Dmitry is among them now, obviously drunk. His hair is slicked back in a way that John knows he could never pull off, and his white dress shirt is so tight that John's sure he can discern the perimeter of his areolae.

"No, I mean, I would refrain from saying hoe, you know what I mean? It's just poor taste," says Dmitry to the red-faced Business major on the adjacent beanbag.

"You don't have to be a particular gender to be a hoe, anyhow," adds one of the RAs as she twists her dreadlocks into a bun.

"Oh, believe me, I know." Dmitry's wrist falls limp as he lets out a devilish giggle.

Again, John finds himself looking for slightly too long. He turns back towards the kitchen, somehow unable to venture further. In the hallway, he sees a lineup for the bathroom and his mind jumps to his full-length mirror and the consolation he might find there. But the thought of retreating to his basement sanctuary when he still has so much momentum feels depressing. He could also try out the upper-level bathroom, and possibly glean secrets about Siyavash or the Mousey Girl from their toiletries or any lingering musks. He knows hummus to be a fickle mistress, and he's not sure how well Siyavash's constitution handles all those biryanis and what-have-yous, especially with all the patriarchal tension he keeps bottled up in his lower abdomen.

A while later the party catches its second wind. People in the living room have started to dance. But there's still no sign of le Kyle, and without their presence, and with Segan still somewhere outside, the vibe inside feels white and apologetic.

John understands that his eye contact with le Kyle last week has given him the license to act as a kind of ethnic proxy, to imbue scenes with flavour, soul, and street credibility whenever he sees fit. And he has a gut feeling that now might be such a time. The more people start to move, the more he feels compelled to do something, to somehow express himself.

Nobody is dancing well enough.

They're all stilted!

John cannot believe for a moment that they're actually having fun and losing themselves in the music as Eminem prescribed circa John's high school days.

Basement Yusef (black-adjacent) is still outside somewhere or else in his room. If he could see what's going on now though, he'd surely agree with John that something isn't right, what with this many Caucasians and model-minorities dancing to hip hop without possessing lived experiences of *The Struggle*.

A lo-fi beat comes on, totally instrumental with a slower tempo than the previous track. John pushes into the crowd and makes a clearing for himself. The song picks up, and he begins to shake his head back and forth, back and forth like a shaman.

"Let's go Foreskin!" somebody yells.

John keeps shaking his head back and forth, back and forth as his knees begin to bounce. The ring of millennials around him begins clapping their hands.

"Come on, Johnny boy!" yells Kerry.

Then John summons the impressions of the rappers he's listened to most over the years. He closes his eyes and grunts a few times, still trying to catch the beat. Finally, he begins to speak, in a cadence distinctly not his own...

I got no filter—like Turkish coffee
You'd think I was out of toner—how I refuse to copy.
Storm warnings—I stay grounded
Like the coffee beans that leave your intesteens
dumbfounded.

I'm confident on every continent
You need Depends to amend your incontinence.

I'm in and out of orifices on official business
With plenty voices in my head I have yet to dismiss.

I get it off my chest like manscaping
and play the field like landscaping.

Like a long-term erection
Who thought I could sustain this?
You've been in a depression
Since you learned what my name is.

Hell ya, your woman's fascinated.
My eyes are shining, son
Been a month since I masturbated.

John falls silent just as the song fades and then changes. It's 50 Cent's *In Da Club*. Everyone in the living room goes wild. John's broken into a cold sweat that he knows signals the shed skin of an inferior form.

All around him is pure hype. Randos cheering and shoving him like in a mosh pit. Kerry is looking at him like she's seeing him for the first time. Even people from the kitchen and hallway have poured in to praise and despise him for ascending beyond his post-colonial whiteness.

He feels liberated from the shackles of the predominating paradigm, exactly like Brad Pitt circa *Fight Club*. As he makes for the kitchen, he observes first the impulse to catch Dmitry's craven eye, and then to search for le Kyle's approving one. He ignores both, knowing that still greater victories lie in waiting. He reaches the sink and splashes water on his face, giving zero thought to how the water might mess up his hair.

An itch at the back of his neck pulls his eyes towards the living room. It's Dmitry. He must have seen the whole thing. John holds his gaze, forbidding himself to smile, and Dmitry looks away first just as John's heart was beginning to burn.

He splashes more water on his face and the back of his neck then finds a clean mason jar in the cupboard and drinks some water. Next, he scarfs down two handfuls of Cheetos and washes them down with coke. Then he takes a shot of whiskey.

When he next looks around, the kitchen is almost empty. He needs a smoke, and to somehow maintain his momentum. He knows the only answer is farming the back porch. There'll be a few people out there who saw his freestyle, and he's finally levelled up enough to stare down whoever's been the alpha out there.

First, he heads to the main floor bathroom for a piss. A few people shout out to him on the way.

The act of peeing while standing up makes him feel powerful like a chad. He washes his hands before, then again afterwards without thinking. The mirror reveals a flush face. And his hair looks good: perfectly greasy, temples properly obscured, scalp scrunched forward to instil vigour into his hairline and make his forehead appear more like a threehead—exactly what everyone else has been seeing for the last few hours.

John Foreskin sees himself winning the struggle against his father, i.e. the struggle against becoming his father. Without regard for who might be waiting outside, he begins feeling up his hairless chest and torso and even slips one hand down his pants to feel the smoothness of his Catholic area. The atlas shower curtain catches his eye and, turning around, he realizes that the *'racsagadam'* he sees every day is actually *Madagascar* spelled backwards. It suddenly feels like everything in his life is coming together.

Exiting the bathroom, he hears familiar voices coming down the stairwell. He doesn't want to look—but he does—and catches le Kyle's eye, then Kerry's. He knows he has to say something.

"Hey guys."

Weak.

"Sup Foreskin?" asks le Kyle.

"You finally made it."

Are you keeping tabs on him?

"Not in time for your performance, I hear. Wish I could have been there, bro."

"Oh…yeah. That happened, I guess."

Good. Downplay it.

"You should have seen it, le Kyle," says Kerry. "John has bars."

John searches le Kyle's eyes.

Did I imagine the entire thing last week?

Was it all just the weed?

He looks away, afraid of more eye contact.

Why do I feel craven?

He is—They're— riding high on something though…

Have they just committed the violent, colonialist act of vaginal penetration?

But then… wouldn't it be WPR?[15]

Is Kerry's face flush?

John looks again into le Kyle's eyes but doesn't see the prideful glint of recent sexual conquest.

"What are you up to now, John?" asks Kerry, jumping down the final few steps.

"I was just heading out for a smoke. Maybe I'll catch you guys back in here?"

"Maybe," answers le Kyle with a smile.

But John is too blinded by thought to feel the warmth of it. He turns for the porch, hearing Kerry giggle just before the door closes.

Le Kyle always knows…

How to hammer the nail into the coffin.

---

[15] White Pussy Reparations

12

Narcissus

2022

JoIhn Foreskin awakes curled up in a ball, the fire of nicotine withdrawal breathing through his limbs. He checks his phone, then groans and pulls the comforter up over his shoulder.

His FTLIJGF—who is a fully autonomous being unto herself—is sprawled across the bed, making the usual chomping and clicking sounds that tell John Foreskin something and nothing about her subconscious. His default posture of envy justifies the conclusion that she enjoys much deeper sleep than he and that he should allow himself to relax and fall back into his dreams. He also wants to stave off his morning stimulants for as long as possible. Six hours of sleep *is* enough though, if not for the limp-wristed wasteman, then for the industrious adult male.

Last night's dreams featured men from John's past, boys from his elementary school days all grown up and in their thirties. He spent most of the night examining their hairlines and drawing conclusions about their lifestyles, willpower, virtue, and genetics.

Shared goals and, paradoxically, competition, reliably evoke the feelings of brotherhood that John Foreskin so longs for and that he knows rough and tumble play is supposed to foster—the play that threatens sodomy, thereby ultimately promoting vaginal intercourse with cis hetero females. But in daily life, where men jealously guard their females while vying for advanced stations, brotherhood takes a back seat to the split-second sizing-up that determines the alpha-beta dynamic of every silent, inter-male elevator ride.

Are men excused from this dance once they've fulfilled nature's prerogative?

Do those breeders even care about their hairlines?

John's mind jumps to his old neighbourhood, to weary forty-somethings watching their young children at play in Edmonds Park. John was single, a renter, lonely, and angry at the world, i.e. he could not walk through the park without those parents regarding him as a potential pedophile.

Being single and in one's thirties is one thing. Being single and poor and male and white is another. And being male and white, and straight and cis, what reasonable excuse could John conjure for being poor?

It seemed to John a dirty trick by Nature, to make those park dads feel so fulfilled despite their waning vitality, just so they'd ensure the developing ones received the proper nourishment and more than enough love, and that they weren't murdered, sold, abandoned, or eaten for being so cunning and hungry all the time.

Unable to stem the flow of his thoughts, John Foreskin rolls out of bed, grabs his vape pen off the dresser, and staggers into the bathroom, leaving the light off so as not to be sucked into the mirror.

He empties his bladder sitting down, but it occurs to him that he should have remained standing because subtle tweaks like this could be the key to revitalizing his sex life. If he feels masculine and virile at every moment, if he fosters gruffness and suspends oxygen in his upper lungs to achieve the archetypical v-frame of the adult alpha male, then he would perhaps be less prone to regression, less prone to regarding his FTLI-JGF as a surrogate mother, more prone to vigorous thrusting, and less prone to pathetic suckling.

Pee finished, he drags himself past the mirror and into the kitchen. He mixes almond milk with yesterday's coffee and nukes it for two minutes, knowing perfectly well how this would dismay his person-of-colour friend whose whose identity also happens to pass through the intersection of

```
                        b
o   v   e   r   e   d   u   c   a   t   e   d
                        r
                    m   i   l   l   e   n   n   i   a   l
                        s
                        t
                        a
```

He takes his mug onto the balcony and finally exhales pomegranate-orange into an impersonal, mechanistic universe.

The sun is just beginning to rise, setting aglow a dense fog that obscures even the neighbouring apartment buildings. John Foreskin suspends thought long enough to hear the cars speeding along wet cement twenty-six floors below. Looking south, he can just make out the blinking runway lights of YVR airport.

Somewhere past those lights, a ninety-minute ferry ride away, is Vancouver Island, where two cousins John never talks to live with their partners and young children. He wonders when he lost touch with them and what he might have said or done, or not said and not done. The funerals and weddings he chose not to attend. The emails he read but never replied to.

How did I become so isolated?

Who do I actually know in Vancouver?

Besides his FTLIJGF, the people John talks to most are all students of his. He looks north-west, in the general direction of West Point Grey. The last ten years have faded into a fog. He has coworkers, but he's never talked to them outside of work. He can count at most two IRL friends, whom he sees only a few times each year, and whom he keeps, for reasons unarticulated, at arms length. He keeps in touch with exactly one friend from Ottawa, via WhatsApp. But he has his girlfriend. And he has his apartment. He has enough.

The FTLIJGF wakes up and greets John with a hug. John offers baby talk, then prepares a breakfast of Polish sausage, egg rolls, hash browns, rice, miso soup, fruit, nattō, and coffee. They eat until they're both suffering, vaping, and life-weary. She dresses and leaves shortly afterwards.

John Foreskin nicotates himself in the comfort of his furnished rental apartment, caffeinates himself in his high-rise, fob-accessed, Vancouver apartment, begins to crown from over-excitement in his balconied, thus-far-afforded, live-in-girlfriend apartment.

Shut the fuck up and die.

Healthy self-talk is important.

Three minutes later: The demon has been expunged. But don't call it a morning miscarriage because that's offensive to women. All men ever have to do is ejaculate like self-serving savages. And the jaundiced glint of their semen betrays their sins.

Luckily some magical tablets from Japan have helped to regulate things. Even though today's business came on urgently, the cleanup was more dignified than yesterday's. The dignity that affords the gratitude that staves off the shame.

John's FTLIJGF has no digestive troubles. She is of hardy stock, is not sent reeling by her iced americanos. Only the whites raised on fruit roll-ups, fruit loops, fruit-by-the-foots, and other faux fruits suffer nervous frailty in early adulthood and require a blood sugar fix following every micro-aggression and crowded elevator ride. Blame the parents for that, and for affording houses. Meanwhile, Jordan B. Peterson can shove responsibility up his white man's rectal cavity.

But sudden crowning is still sudden crowning, and John Foreskin wonders what the state of his bowels will be by the time he reaches old age, the indignities he'll suffer, the pity he'll receive from care staff—who by then will likely all be disgruntled, low-income, cisgender white males who've failed to adapt to the fallen patriarchy.[16]

John pictures himself walking by the old folks home in Edmonds, back when he lived with reprobate, obese Mitch, before he got his new apartment. His smiles were always pity smiles. Pity masking self-pity.

John knew those old folks were doing their laps of the block to promote continence. They'd walk by his house sometimes, too. He used to watch them, from his basement window, as his muscles atrophied, as he shivered from his iced lattes, as he clenched against the impending exodus, as they strived in the morning sun against death and time, as he questioned the use of striving for anything. The old neighbourhood where he was a mere renter of a room on a street of giant, multi-million-dollar houses. He was a second-class citizen, walking home with heavy grocery bags past tinted Teslas and every kind of luxury SUV.

The indignity of exertion for an audience.

Second class.

Now John Foreskin has his own apartment with a fob-activated elevator. But he still feels like he doesn't belong, like at any moment he'll wake up in his damp basement room, sharing a toilet seat with balding Mitch, turning up the volume on his laptop speakers to

---

[16] e.g. by transitioning

drown out his asinine Boomer phone conversations about Fox News and Nancy Pelosi.

It suddenly occurs to John that he will never have to smell Mitch's adult male digestive shame again.

The indignity of shared adult quarters.

The indignity of an already-warm toilet seat.

Half the thumbnails on John's YouTube front page reinforce a paradigm of productivity and dopamine levels. As he exercises his adult right to vape, the sounds of the busy intersection remind him that it is noon on a weekday.

Following several more minutes of desperate, post-coffee YouTube browsing, he resolves to dress quickly and avoid any more of the haunting that takes place when he's alone in the apartment.

I'll hand out business cards!

I need to start attracting more clients anyways.

What he needs to do is increase the frequency of the e-transfers that stave off the sweating and truncated lifespan associated with financial insecurity.

Adult male industry.

On the way to the bedroom, he passes his unposing self in the bathroom mirror and catches a glimpse of the sheer villainy in his face.

Self-pity is my deepest stroke of cunning.

The thought feels tweetable. But *not* tweeting it feels somehow more mature.

John Foreskin waits on the northbound skytrain platform at Marine Drive Station without knowing exactly where he's heading. He happens to look up from his phone towards the opaque, grey sky, and, for a thoughtless moment, he actually sees it.

The sky.

The contortion performed by his facial muscles reminds him of how he feels about his life, how he's felt for a long time.

Immersion in the scientific-materialist paradigm is the surest way to forget the inherently personal quality of the Universe. But this immersion does not undo the fact that a human being either is or is not grateful to be alive. It does not undo the fact that a human being either does or does not blame the Universe for the suffering their life entails.

The skytrain is crowded with students and construction workers. The construction workers mostly wear bandanas instead of regular face masks.[17] They look to

---

[17] During the global pandemic of Covid-19, people wore face masks in an attempt to reduce the spread of the virus, or in some cases to avoid ostracism and/or arrest.

John like criminals, and the Caucasian ones like potential white supremacists.

He gets off at King Edward and starts walking towards Main Street, wishing he was walking *with* the wind so that his bangs wouldn't fly everywhere.

Since you were about to ask, the precise moment when John Foreskin began obsessing over his hairline arrived on the morning of the first day of grade seven. He was standing in front of the basement half-bath vanity at 3344 Uplands Drive, applying Dippity-Do hair gel for the very first time…

He had got his hair cut at the end of that summer from a 90s-style mushroom to something shorter that all the dark-haired Italian and Lebanese boys at school were sporting, and that required hair gel to stick up and actually look cool.

As he combed back his bangs for the first time, he was met by a certain m-shaped precociousness.

The horror.

However, it would be incorrect to say that John Foreskin fell *immediately* into despair, for of course there was that moment. You know the one. For it is afforded to every human being in such straits. There was the moment when he was presented with the choice of whether to care.

And of course, we already know what John Foreskin chose. He chose to care, and so to add his hairline to the existing evidence that the Universe, or perhaps the Abrahamic God, had so forsaken him that he could not possibly be grateful for his life.

And so a new heaviness was born in his chest that day, to dwell among the other heavinesses that he (in so far as he harboured them) regarded as his lot.

And so it was that the basement half-bath became his private chamber of vanity, the mirror an altar of sacrifice whereupon each morning he would offer up any zest for life that he might have woken up with.

John Foreskin would likely lead a more productive life, in the adulting-under-capitalism sense of the term, and a more meaningful life, in the Jordan B. Peterson sense of the term,
    if he were not this obsessed with his hair,
    if he were not so convinced of the evil of balding,
    of the proof that balding is of the evil of men,
    of the proof that balding is of one's own evil.

But long before that morning, on the first day of grade seven, John Foreskin knew, to close his eyes, what lay above them. Just as he now knows, at the age of thirty-something, when he closes his eyes and finally settles the chatter, that the webs of his cunning remain, inside his temples, even the ones he spun all the way back in elementary school when he already knew for a fact that even though nobody else knew his secrets, the Universe still knew them, when he sensed for a fact, like every child on the face of the Earth senses, that he was never truly alone.

John turns left onto Ontario Street and heads towards the side streets where he and his FTLIJGF always walk together. It's easier to think and vape here, plus the houses offer some shelter from the wind.

He begins picturing Main Street and the cafés where he might possibly leave some business cards.

If I could only secure one or two more regular students.

Yet it also occurs to him that Main Street may be altogether too Caucasian for what he has in mind: farming the Chinese diaspora's profound disappointment in the Canadian public school system.

He posts up at Main & 21st near a Thai place that he's been meaning to try. He passes a few minutes vaping before finally taking the stack of business cards out of his coat pocket.

A pair of Jehovah's Witnesses are set up across the street with their stand of booklets.

John projects pity and mild discomfort onto the people walking past them.

A couple approaches on his side of the street and a lump begins to form in his throat. They pass without looking at him.

An SUV pulls up, and a man exits, Ubereats bag in hand. He walks past John and enters the Thai place.

I could be delivering food right now.

Yea, if you had a fucking driver's licence.

Cars whizz by the corner. Countless people with driver's licences, going about their business, following their dreams, or at least earning enough money to support their families.

What the fuck is wrong with me?

I need to work more.

Maybe one of the academies can offer me more classes.

John whips out his phone and checks his inbox.

Fund Transfer Notice
no.reply.hk@sc.com
Dear JOHN,
ZHOU WEI YONG has initiated a transfer of CAD 3,000.00 to your bank account in TD BANK on 23/11/2022.

Please check your account later to confirm funds receipt.

Yours sincerely,
Standard Chartered Bank (Hong Kong) Limited

John Foreskin strolls along Main Street having forgotten all about his aspirations of adult male industry. He now feels the kind of zest for life that is so often accompanied by the spontaneous desire to spend money. He ducks into a café and orders a warmed-up to-go croissant, plus a kind of 'why-not' half-sweet iced mocha, effectively challenging the Universe to prove there's such a thing as too much caffeine.

A few doors down, he gets a wiener bun and a pack of frozen croquettes from this quaint Asian grocer that still sells DVDs. In his interactions with the baristas and shop clerks, he exudes ease and Trudeauian beneficence.

The wind is against his back on the way to King Edward. The sky has cleared, and the sun seems to approve of him and the track he's on in life. He can feel his hair properly obscuring his temples and the wind drying the sweat triggered by his human interactions. The business cards are bulging up his pocket, but he pushes them out of his mind, seeking out eye contact with the people he passes while sucking his straw and singing the song that was playing in the café.

"Because I gotta have faith. 'Cause I gotta have faith, faith, faith!"

When he reaches King Edward, he checks his inbox again. His only class of the day has been cancelled.

His evening is now wide open, his screens are waiting for him, and if one of his favourite Twitch streamers is live when he reaches the apartment, it'll feel like fate.

"Before this river...becomes an ocean...I gotta have faith! I gotta have faith, faith, faith! Bayyybeh!"

Jumping down the stairs to the train platform, John Foreskin gives no thought to tomorrow or the next day, nor to how long today's e-transfer will last him, nor to how he'll feel about his life once he's come down from his current high.

13

Creature of Habit

2012

John hasn't seen anyone important since the party though yesterday he heard co-ed blitz chess coming from the living room and felt certain Kerry and le Kyle were among the gathering.

Ever since the party he's been using nicotine and, more problematically, refined sugars to fend off thoughts of RCIC[18] a.k.a. White Pussy Reparations.[19] Meanwhile, his shorn body is still paying dividends, especially during visits to Starbucks where he now feels comfortable:

- rubbing his non-erogenous zones as a form of self-care
- standing up perfectly straight, and
- performing stretches that expose his midriff

---

[18] Reverse Colonial Interracial Coitus
[19] Both subcategories of BBC

This morning he was woken up by the sound of AHF[20] coming from two floors above him—male bestiality eliciting female whimpers. This was followed by the unmistakable sound of male vulnerability, typically indicative of one or more fingers up the bum—the fingers that elicit the whimpers that exorcise the toxic masculinity.

John Foreskin considers Starbucks. He knows he'll go eventually. But gratitude feels far away and impossible, so he also knows how badly the sun will make him pay this morning, how much he'll sweat from his catholic area (manscaped or not) before he even reaches the café and how soon afterwards he'll need to shit out his entire torso.

Too much from deep inside has been roused, ever since the party, too much that the sun can punish him for. Plus he hasn't been using his exercise bike at all, and he can't find his red Swedish pullover anywhere. He knows he's too weak to face any human that he already knows.

He thinks about the Center and the money he's wasting by not going. He misses Dudek sometimes, too. His warmth, and the way he doesn't seem to want anything, other than to help. He's called twice, since John's first visit, but John never picked up, and he

---

[20] Aggressive Hetero Fornication

stopped calling after that. He feels bad about it, but he knows that entering that house means…facing himself. And that's the last thing he wants to do, even if deep down he knows it's what he needs the most.

Then he hatches a plan:

1. Dress in clothing that conveys not trying.
2. Pack a bag, including new moleskin and go-to felt-tip pen, just in case the mood strikes.
3. Rinse face.
4. Dampen hair with indirect water contact, i.e. by wetting hands.
5. Freshen up still-smooth-AF twenty-something male Caucasian body, focusing on the armpits and catholic area.
6. Walk extra far to an unknown café that I'm sure my walk will lead me to.

He mounts the basement stairs two at a time then pauses in the kitchen to feel out the house. A soft, whiny falsetto drifts in from the living room. It's a man's voice delivering a gospel rendition of the all-bro kitchen mantra:

"Fear the stick, my *brotha*. Fear the *sti-ee-yi-ee-yick.*"

John recognizes Dmitry's voice and fights back a smile.

He reaches the bathroom and locks the door without looking into the living room. Given that it's still morning, Dmitry is likely caffeinated, so John knows he can't take too long. He follows steps 3, 4, and 5 of his P.O.A.[21] while doing his best not to get sucked into the mirror. He can still hear Dmitry singing.

When he exits the bathroom, Dmitry is standing in the center of the living room performing wide-legged squats with a mug in one hand and an unlit cigarette in the other. His jeans are Euro-tight, and his button-up is club-ready.

"Hey, Johnny Boy the freestyler. Gymnastics to strengthen the sinews of the soul, am I right?"

John heads for the kitchen.

Dmitry meets him there via the living room. "Plato, bro. I thought you were a Philosophy major."

"Oh. Right." John grabs a mason jar from the cupboard and runs the tap.

"Yeah, I took the day off," says Dmitry, nonchalantly. "Self-care basically. It's good to just reset, you know?"

"I feel you."

John wipes his mouth and adds the mason jar to the pile of dishes in the sink.

"Fear the stick, Johnny boy," says Dmitry with a devilish grin.

"Yeah, yeah."

---

[21] Plan of action

"No worries, bro. Most of those are Yusef's, actually. By the way, have you seen le Kyle? I can't get hold of them. We were supposed to work out today. Chest, I think."

"Probably with Kerry." John steals another glance at Dmitry's dress shirt. The guy's built like a boxer.

Dmitry sucks his teeth. "Yeah, those two seem very buddy-buddy lately. I don't get it to be honest."

"Kerry left at 9:15 this morning. She has Mondays off. Le Kyle has class until 1:30." Mousey girl has procured her hummus from the fridge and is already walking back to the front stairwell, bare feet slapping against the hardwood.

"Thanks?" Dmitry calls after her before following John out back and lighting his cigarette. "Where the fuck did she come from?"

John shakes his head. "What's her name again?"

"Cynthia, I think. Her room is right next to mine. But I never hear a sound from her. Smoke?"

"I'm good."

Dmitry breaks into song: "Fear the stick, my *brotha*. Fear the *sti-ee-yi-ee-yick*."

John shakes his head, trying not to smile.

"Boss remix, eh?"

"By the way, what kind of name is *Dudek* you think? Russian?"

Dmitry frowns. "Dudek? Non monsieur, not Russian. Could be Polish. Or Czech maybe. Why?"

"Just wondering. But yeah, I gotta go, man." John jumps down the porch stairs.

"Just wondering, eh?" mutters Dmitry, and then, calling after him: "John, wait."

John turns around. "What is it?"

Dmitry exhales sideways, scrunching up his face. "I know what you have in your room, bro. I'm just saying."

"What?"

"The exercise bike. I saw you that night. You didn't see me, but I saw you."

"Okay... So what?"

"So, it always feels like you're holding back around me, John. Like you have secrets."

John's throat dries up.

"Trust me, I know what that feels like. And it isn't easy."

"I don't—I'm late, man. I gotta go." He makes for the laneway.

"All good, brother. I'm just saying. I'm here. If you ever wanna talk. Fear the stick, John!" Dmitry calls after him. "Fear the stick!"

Time to walk. Single-minded purpose galvanizes the mojo. Cigarette before any caffeine or food. Pure majesty. Then it's kegels for ten blocks in the name of adult-male dignity.

"Fear the stick, my brotha, fear—"

Fucking Dmitry.

What the fuck was he—

I just don't get—

Why is he—

He's obsessed with le Kyle.

What secrets does he think I have?

What secrets does HE have?

Familiar streets. Then new ones. The houses imply innumerable lives and innumerable subjective experiences, e.g. people who wear wrap-around sunglasses and drive old Volkswagen Westfalias to music festivals and mountain trails, mountains that John might glimpse if he ever bothered to look up at the horizon.

Leaving navigation to karma, he ends up at Broadway & Granville. Boomers and senior millennials with their shit together are out on lunch breaks from legitimate office jobs. John's entire vagabond aesthetic feels like a mistake now. Even smoking feels frowned upon here. There's a Starbucks though, attached to the Indigo bookstore.

What—

The actual—

Fuck.

Kerry is standing outside the Starbucks. She's wearing a green cardigan over a white blouse with a skirt that ends a few inches above her knees. And she's with Dudek, handing out pamphlets.

John slows his pace, but he's already been spotted.

"Yo Johnny boy." Kerry fist-pumps John's shoulder.

"Kerry. Hey. What are you doing here?"

"I'm just hanging out. Thanks to you, kind of."

"Me?"

"You already know Dudek, eh?"

"Hallo, brother."

They shake hands.

So light.

John remembers how empty the Center felt, how Dudek and Hyemin were able to sneak up on him. "What do you mean, thanks to me?" John says, turning back to Kerry.

"The pamphlet for the Center. It was in your hoodie pocket."

John blinks

"From the party?"

"Oh, right…"

"Isn't that great, John? And now Kerry is helping with promotion."

"Oh my god, John. How drunk were you? You lent me your hoody in the backyard, remember? The red one you're like literally always wearing. I found the pamphlet in the front pocket."

John's mind flashes back to the night of the party, to Kerry leaning against the bannister, beside le Kyle.

Was she already wearing it then?

Did she show the pamphlet to le Kyle?

Kerry and Dudek are smiling like they know something John doesn't.

"I went three days ago," says Kerry. "To the Center. I love it there. The vibe is—well yea. I guess you already know."

"Right…the vibe."

Kerry and Dudek won't stop smiling.

"So now what, John?" asks Dudek. "Starbucks?"

"Yeah." John forces a laugh.

"Did you walk all the way here from West Point Grey, John?"

"Yeah. Needed to clear my head."

Dudek cocks back his head and laughs.

"He's always walking, aren't you, John?"

"Walking is fantastic exercise," says Dudek. "And the colours of the fall, beautiful…just beautiful."

"For sure," says John.

"What is that? Is that a chipmunk?"

"That's a squirrel."

"Ah, yes. Squeerrel," repeats Dudek. "Busy preparing for winter. We are all *so* busy, yes?"

John looks at the ground.

"Well, we're gonna be out here for a while longer. Right, Dudek?"

"That's right, Krry. She is such a great helper, John."

"Well, I'm gonna head in," says John, with an apologetic smile.

"Come with us, John! I want to meditate with you!"

"We'll see."

It's the lunch rush inside the Starbucks, but the interaction outside has made John practically invincible. As he waits for his drink, he feels strangely at ease. He corrects his posture to a chad-like verticality that denotes zero intention to subordinate himself to top-heavy bros named Bret or Christian. Then, without thinking, he switches his knapsack to his front side, clasping his hands together over the top, and watches, in a state of near rapture, as the barista deftly prepares his drink. What John Foreskin has failed to notice (bless his soul) is that he has, since entering the Starbucks, entertained no notion of how he might appear to others.

Turning to the community board, he sees one of the meditation pamphlets pinned up with a magnet. It's different from the one Dudek gave him a few weeks ago, but the words seem more or less the same:

Find your true mind: The Universe Mind
Live a True Life
The Method

Free Introductory Seminar

He checks the back. It's the same stick man drawing with the oversized head.

Why does that picture make me feel so sad?

What—

A firm pat on the back.

"Hallo, John."

"S-sup!"

How does he keep doing that?

Dudek is walking past him to the exit, and he's come *from* the bathrooms, apparently, but John didn't even see him go in.

"Iced latte for John," calls the Barista.

"Iced latte for John." Dudek mimics, spinning around with sudden grace. "John, the creature of habit!"

"Heh, yeah."

There's a slight lull in the café buzz as people turn to look, but John doesn't feel the least bit embarrassed. Dudek spins back around and exits.

He feels good.

His pat on the back…

It felt…

It still feels…

Like le Kyle.

John looks around the café. A table's just opened up, but his legs don't move. He looks back outside. It's a beautiful sunny day. And he can see Kerry. She's smiling.

◆

Dudek sits in the corner of the meditation room on the first floor of the house on Balaclava Street. His head is bowed, and his legs are tucked under his bottom.

Another man, who introduced himself as Adam, paces at the front of the room, his ignobly low hairline and ambiguous ethnicity lending a kind of primal credence to everything he says.

"It's about polarity, brothers and sisters, about balancing, one proposition against another. Because it *is* a proposition, is it not? That simple sentence, consisting of a subject and a verb: *I exist.* Say it with me, everyone."

"I exist."

A dozen or so people sit cross-legged on cushions.

"So it's not about *denying* that you exist, and it's also not about *depriving* your senses," explains Adam with air quotes. "You can exist, and then you can *believe* that you exist, maintaining that belief, holding onto it for dear life. Two very different things. Are you guys still with me?"

"Yes," says a man seated near the front.

"So this meditation is about ceasing or at least suspending that belief, which really, if you think about it, is the foundational premise of all your mental chatter. Suspend that one belief, and see what happens."

They break for coffee and snacks. John's sure he heard someone in the kitchen during the lecture, and now sandwiches and cookies have appeared on the island. But still no sign of the lady from John's first visit.

Kerry invited le Kyle as well, and they picked them up with Dudek's car in Point Grey before heading back to the Centcr. Le Kyle and Dudek enjoyed seamless bro talk the entire way.

Now le Kyle's chatting up some *having-read-Eckhart-Tolle* boomers. He sees John and smiles. John smiles back, but he can't shake the thought that he said something stupid at the party.

How drunk was I?

Do they know Dmitry was looking for them earlier?

Mind your own fucking business.

Don't be desperate.

He enters the hallway. The hardwood floor is immaculate, like the rest of the house. He pokes his head back in the meditation room. Adam and Dudek are perched on their cushions like origami cranes, nodding as Kerry speaks in a hushed tone.

He walks on before they see him. His own exchanges with Dudek always make him feel like he's held something back. Dudek's always got this expectant smile on his face, like he's giving John an opportunity to open up. The other one, Adam, hasn't so much as made eye contact with him yet.

Why does that make me feel craven?

He passes back through the kitchen. People are snacking and chatting away. Nobody takes particular notice of him, and he suddenly feels the urge to check his reflection. He heads for the hallway bathroom. An older man beats him to it though, meeting his eyes before closing the door. Wandering further down the hall, he finds another room, its door slightly ajar, and steps in.

It's dim and empty except for a stack of cushions in the corner and a large whiteboard on the wall opposite the window. There's also a door to what John supposes is a closet. The room is large enough to be a bedroom, except that it's on the main floor, so it may have originally been an office. The sheen on the hardwood and the absence of furniture give it that same air of immaculate cleanliness, and there's a stillness here as well, distinct from the hallway, that seems to accentuate the sound of John's thoughts.

The window faces the backyard of the house, where John can see neatly cut grass, a wooden picnic table, and a sizable vegetable garden retained by scrap planks of wood.

Just then, a tall, slender figure donning a sunhat enters the frame of John's view and approaches the garden. John immediately recognizes her as the woman from his first visit.

From the middle of the dark room, he watches as she crouches and begins picking vegetables from the garden and dropping them into a large, metal bucket. The vegetables appear to be green peppers, which she picks with a subtle flick of her wrists, employing both hands with equal dexterity. When she finishes one area, she grabs the bucket by the handle, rises from her crouched position, strides exactly one pace, and crouches again, flicking aside the handle to *clank* against the side of the bucket. John looks on, intrigued by the deftness of her movements and recalls again how she and Dudek were able to sneak up on him during his first visit. His mind jumps to how empty this house must feel once all the students have gone home, even if Dudek, Adam, and the lady in the garden all live here together. And he's somehow convinced they do.

Just as he catches himself, his head abuzz, the woman turns and looks directly at the window. Her eyes shouldn't be able to pierce the darkness of the room, but she keeps looking, straight at John, as if her work was disturbed by the sound of his thoughts.

John steps first backward, then out of her line of sight. Suddenly hot, he edges closer to the wall and remains still until hearing what sounds like the resumption of her work.

He notices the silence of the room again, his breathing, and then his sweaty palms against the wall. Turning around, he sees a black and white poster that he didn't notice before. It's the same stick figure drawing as the meditation pamphlets. The figure's attitude is downcast, its oversized head tilting forward. A collection of items floats inside its head: a dollar sign, a heart, a stick figure family, a skull. The stick man stands alone, inside a circle, somehow reminding John of *Le Petit Prince*. Outside the circle, a group of smaller stick figures stand smiling, with open arms and slitted eyes.

Their heads are empty and in proportion to their bodies, and they're surrounded by animals, trees, mountains, and the sun, who also smiles, as it shines down upon them.

Another *clank* from the garden pulls John's attention back into the room. He heads for the door, then stops and opens the closet.

The inside is jam-packed: cardboard boxes, a bent hula hoop, a folding table, what looks like a rolled-up projector screen. Stuffed in between the larger items are all kinds of folders and loose papers. The whole mess looks like it could burst into the room at any moment.

John lifts the flap on one of the boxes. It's full of pamphlets, the same as he was given. He checks another box, then another. More pamphlets. The first two are labelled "Vancouver West Side: November." A third is labelled December. Each box must contain at least five hundred. His mind jumps to the dozen or so people attending today's lecture, then to the hundreds of pamphlets that must get thrown in the trash each month, in Vancouver West alone. The top shelf is packed with shoe boxes and papers ready to fall all over him. He shuts the closet door just as a voice calls out from down the hall.

"The cameras on your phones—did each of you know that the camera was designed according to the principles of the human eye? The human body *is* a camera, brothers and sisters. Please consider. And not just *eyes*. All five senses. With five senses, we take pictures, detailed pictures, of world." Dudek pauses and cracks a crooked smile. "Let us try something together. Please, everyone, close eyes."

John closes his eyes, unable to stop the smile spreading across his face.

"Can you imagine the room we are in now?"

"Yes!" says le Kyle, almost shouting.

The entire group giggles.

"Good!" Dudek replies, matching le Kyle's energy. "Now, you have sense of lighting. You have sense of who is around you. Where *Adam* is sitting in the corner, where Kerry sits. And John."

John feels himself blush.

"That image exists. In some sense. But in other sense, maybe we say it does not? You can imagine it because five senses have taken detailed pictures. And when your eyes close you can still see it. Correct?"

"Correct."

"Correct."

"Sozen, we ask the question: *where* do you live? *Where* are you living now? In real world? Are you living in this room? In this house? On Balaclava Street? Or, are you living in picture of that room, of this house, picture taken with five senses and then stored inside your mind? Which now even with eyes closed, you update with other four senses. And what about, brothers and sisters, when you open your eyes? Zen, are you seeing the world, or are you still seeing picture that you can see now with eyes closed?"

A few thoughtful grunts as people shift on their cushions.

"Now, open your eyes."

John opens them, not quite sure he's followed Dudek's logic.

"If you look for zem, you *will* find pictures of not just this room but *every* room of your life. That is because human body is camera. H*uman body is camera*," Dudek repeats, punching fist into palm with each word. "And your life has been stored inside that camera.

"We are creatures of habit, brothers and sisters. This picture-taking is habit of humans. Some of you are here today because you have begun to feel the weight of that habit, of all those pictures. Even from a young age, you can feel. Sozen, do we continue accumulation? Like picture squeerrel preparing for picture winter." Dudek flashes his crooked teeth at John.

"With the *Method,* you will learn to remove pictures. That is what we are going to do today. Sozen! Is everyone ready to begin?"

"Ready, captain!"

The group cracks up. It was Kerry this time. Dudek only smiles and shakes his head.

John dares a look backward. Adam's still seated in the corner, head bowed.

"Sounds like you have eaten too many of Hyemin's cookies," exclaims Dudek.

More laughter.

"Okay! Brothers and sisters! This is time for focus. Close eyes. And breathe deeply. Relax your body and assume a *righteous* posture."

John looks around as the others settle down, then closes his eyes, feeling his chin tuck in as his spine straightens. The group falls still, and John begins to withdraw into his body, deeper and deeper, as if *he* is shrinking while his body remains the same.

Dr. Varma's report springs into his mind: *"Deep body absorption."*

He tries focusing on the room: its walls, the ceiling, the dimming daylight. It's all there, when he looks for it, images captured by his senses that now define the boundary of his inner reality. Dudek's words are starting to make some sense.

For a few moments, there is silence. Then, from behind them, a voice begins to speak:

"This, my friends, is the Method."

The words send a shiver through John's body.

"For now," continues Adam, "keep your eyes closed, and try to follow along as best you can."

A few more seconds pass as people get comfortable on their cushions. From behind his eyelids, John notices the lights dim.

When Adam next speaks, his voice sounds deeper, more hollow:

"This is a real situation. Let's truly die."

Part two

A House with Levels

14

The Method

2012

"You are walking along a busy city sidewalk. You can feel the concrete beneath your feet. You can see the towering buildings all around you, the shadows they cast. People brush your shoulders as they walk past. Drivers honk their horns. Countless people going about their lives. And it's all beautiful. So beautiful. You're having a good day. And you're on your way to meet a good friend.

"Suddenly, you become aware of commotion up ahead. People begin to point and scream. They're running towards you, and before you know it you've been swept up in the crowd, pushed along without knowing why.

"You turn and look just as a skyscraper collapses, swallowed up by a giant fissure that is spreading toward you! You try to run faster, to push your way through the sea of people. But try as you might, you're stuck! And then it's too late. The fissure swallows you up, along with the rest of the crowd, and you fall for a long, long time.

Down

down

down you go,

deep into the Earth.

Down

down

down,

until finally, everything just goes dark.

"Next thing you know, you're walking down a long hallway. At the end, two big doors open before you. At first, you can't see anything. It's all too bright. But things slowly come into focus.

"Figures. A group of people standing together. You realize that it's a funeral. And as you begin to recognize the faces of the people, you realize it's *your* funeral. Your friends and family are all there, heads bowed. Some are crying. Others are deep in thought. You try talking to them, but they can't hear you. You try touching them, but they can't feel you.

"It is then that you realize…you have died. It is then that you realize you have become a ghost."

There's a pause, and John notices how tense he's become in the buttocks and shoulders.

"I've died, you think to yourself. And you realize there's nothing left for you on the Earth. So you make up your mind to leave." The tone of Adam's voice suddenly shifts.

"I begin going up

up

up

up

up into space. I leave the atmosphere of the Earth and continue going

up

up

up

up until the Earth is the size of a quarter.

I keep going

up

up

up!

"Finally, I stop. And I float here, alone, in the middle of the emptiness…

"Nothing much is going on, and Earth is a *tiny* spot lightyears away. All around me is blackness. Stillness.

Distant stars twinkle, but I am all alone with nothing but my memories, my thoughts, and my feelings.

"Time passes this way. It passes and it passes, without much of anything changing around me. But the memories, the thoughts, and the feelings remain.

"And that's when I realize something. I realize that they are all inside of *me* and that they all came from the life I lived *so* long ago on the Earth that is now *so* far away.

"And at that very moment, a black hole appears before me and I understand something. I understand that I can let go of everything I'm holding onto and throw it all into the black hole. The black hole will suck it all up, leaving me completely…empty…."

Another pause.

"Now, open your eyes."

John slowly cracks his eyes open to discover a line of small black circles stuck to the wall at eye level. He focuses on the hole directly in front of him, resisting the urge to look around.

"Now, beginning from the earliest memory you can think of, begin bringing up everything in your life, little by little, in chronological order, and throw each memory into the black hole. Once you've let it go, it's gone forever. And remember: I've died. I've become a ghost. I'm completely alone. I've been floating here for hundreds if not thousands of years. And the Earth is millions of lightyears away."

Adam steps out of sight, and a few moments later comes the rushing of the kitchen tap. The water's flow carries John away...

He finds himself in the first home he can remember, in Ottawa. Rochester street. Cartoons on the TV. Eating his mom's grilled cheese. He always sat on the far left side of the white couch. He felt like a king on that couch...

Then to Uplands Drive. First arriving. And a heaviness. Something he'd carried inside from Rochester had followed him there. A spectre three stories high. But what was it?

Then the basement, and the old white couch again. At certain parts, you could fall right through to the cold, tiled floor. And all the crumbs and loose change. And jumping on it with his cousin Christine while singing "I feel like Chicken tonight, like Chicken tonight!" And the feeling of not knowing what "Ragu" was on the TV, but still loving that song. They kept jumping up and down, up and down, singing the jingle over and over. He wanted to stop! He wanted everything to just calm down!

Because...

Because I never wanted to lose control.

Then it was daycare. And more control. Keeping up
his guard. Counting to one million at nap time just so
he wouldn't fall asleep. Feeling his heart swell, but
never allowing it to open up. Never completely.

John feels so hot. Too hot. But the memories keep
bubbling up.

Then to the schoolyard, recess, and getting punched
in the stomach. He'd coveted the boy's sister. But why?
Because his own mother wasn't there. But the boy
knew. Strong and stupid. But he knew. And his actual
name was *Chad.*

The proto-chad at the beginning of all the chads…

So many memories.

So many secrets.

The past is…

Inside of me.

John Foreskin snaps out of it. Silence surrounds him.
Thick. Poised. It has always been there, he knows, ever
since he was a boy. But now he can feel it again, like it's
alive. Though, it occurs to him, he's not perfectly sure
of its intentions. He wipes sweat from his brow before
noticing how much his head is aching.

Just like the first time.

The memories came from his gut, it felt like, and
rose up, before exiting from a spot between his eyes, a

spot that now feels...clogged. The memories were... gelatinous. Not quite material, yet...unmistakably... there.

John tries again, pacing himself and taking breaks, telling himself to breathe. But he can't find the same pace. Whatever stream he tapped into has dried up, and the peripheral noises of the house are beginning to distract him.

The next thing he knows, people are standing up. Kerry approaches Dudek in the corner. He stands and they embrace tightly. Something is between them now that John isn't a part of. He looks for le Kyle. He's still seated, eyes closed. He grabs his knapsack and heads for the front door, all the while feeling very light, but tired, and clumsy, like he's forgotten how to walk.

On the front porch, he pats his pockets before asking an older gentleman for a smoke.

"Ah. You were sitting in front of me, I believe. How'd you find the meditation, young man?"

"Ya. Thanks."

"I suppose we'd better smoke these further from the house."

"Ya."

Ya?

Is that all I can say?

They reach the curb and John accepts the man's light.

"First time?"

"Ya. I mean… Yes, technically."

I don't feel like myself.

"I've been at it for, oh, around eight months now? Still in Level 1, mind you. Don't expect too much to change. At least not all at once." He chuckles, a glimmer in his eye.

More people begin trickling out the front door.

John nods, then motions that he's got to go.

The man bows.

He walks north on Balaclava, forming a pensive shield behind his back. The cigarette tastes like shit, but he smokes it greedily.

He's halfway down the street when he looks up from the sidewalk to the pink and orange sky above the horizon. He blinks as the space between his eyes finally unclogs. Then his shield drops and he can feel the street extending backwards behind him. The world around him appears strangely new. He takes another drag of the cigarette and exhales into a Universe that knows his every secret, a Universe that has always known.

Did I *do what just happened?*

Or was it done to me?

He looks again at the horizon.

Nemesis.

You're too low in the sky.

And I've already given enough of myself.

To this…

What did Adam call it?

The method.

Somehow…

Somehow it eases the burden.

The method eases the burden.

◈

Early evening—Christendom Post-Colonial Unceded Territory of the Americas—Café Interior.

Children of Sin imbibe the galvanizing brown brew that sets things off at both ends of the organism. Psychedelic post-funk jungle music helps to soothe white guilt by inclining patrons towards belief in a pre-colonial, pre-Christian time of druidism, a time of harmony with nature when claiming to be something other than a white plague upon the earth might not have constituted cultural appropriation.

Whatever took place earlier, in that house on Balaclava Street, it has somehow put John Foreskin back in touch with a reserve of gut-bound morbidity, which he

now harnesses to counter the syrup-fuelled levity emanating from a group of preteen Frapé Zoomers still
only halfway through their grandes. He presses the
balls of his feet against the floor and manspreads so
that his knees touch the arms of his plush for-here
leather chair. He isn't sweating from any of his usual
areas, and this in spite of his light-iced grande almond
milk latte. And now the following appears true of John
Foreskin's uncircumcised circumstances:

> Premise 1: John is caffeinated, nearly to the
> point of crowning.
>
> Premise 2: He is surrounded by the plush,
> brown leathers of a just-so, for-here café
> interior.
>
> Premise 3: Today's meditation confirmed
> many of the facts of life, facts suppressed
> by the predominating scientific-materialist
> paradigm.
>
> Premise 4: John has with him his new, not to
> be trifled with, nor to be understood by
> boomers, red moleskin notebook.
>
> ∾
>
> Conclusion: John reaches into his pants,
> whips out his felt-tip pen, then begins to
> wax alchemical, sparing grave, sidelong
> glances for only the most comely of café
> nubiles, as well as beta males whom he's

sure he can subordinate with eye contact
alone.

I start out lying flat on my back
my hands by my sides.
I'm intent on letting go of it all.
But every single time it defeats me,
and I finish curled up in a ball.
When I awake, the world mocks me for those parts of it
I've held onto through the night.
And so, I start all over again, but never fresh...
I'm told...
I'm told this is called ageing.

As the majesty of the espresso subsides, John is left
with that unsettled feeling in his stomach, a dry aching
in his adult male's prefrontal cortex, and the certain
knowledge that only a cigarette can sustain the momentum of what is still surely a very young night.

He stuffs his writing implements into his
vagabond's knapsack and heads for the door. During
his just-a-little-too-violent smoking of his second
bummed cigarette, John feels invincible. He is in Vancouver now, not lowly *Ottawa*, where acquaintances or
even an uncle or aunt might catch him exercising his
adult right to smoke.

Now he understands that the only correct continua-
tion to his current streak is to temper cerebral activity

by filling his belly with proteinous (and preferably greasy) food.

Following these stages in proper order,

Adhering to one's metabolism,

Following one's heart, quite in spite of the predominating paradigm,

Riding the highs that permit the deepest of mystical insights,

Attributing these insights to something other than an over-active imagination emergent from an over-caffeinated organism,

Not getting too down about one's messy-as-fuck bowel movements, or what these might indicate about one's diet and lifestyle,

All whilst investing exactly zero thought into one's career path, potential long-term goals, or credit card balance—

This is what the artistic-mystic-vagabond life is all about.

On the way to Safeway John stops at Liberty Wine Merchant where he always buys his Belmont cigarettes. Waiting in line, he finds himself picking up a small bottle of English gin. He palms it thoughtfully, and not asexually, as he reads every single word and number on the label. He intuits that the gin will have a settling effect on his nerves and digestion. Of course, his morning coffee will still rip right through him in a matter of minutes. But picking up the dignified glass bottle with its green tint feels like discovering a fact of life long known to his peers in proto-adulting.

'Well-oiled', John knows, does not simply mean intoxicated, or regularly so. It has to do with a certain facility in life, with darker colouring, and more head grease than his current penchant for potato chips and abstract thought allows. But he likes the idea of being well-oiled. It has to do with sternness, and with one's kidneys, and with Brad Pitt circa *always*. Most kept men are well-oiled, and a surprising number of Japanese as well. But John is fair haired and flighty, and spicy foods send him reeling. The gin can only ever mitigate these symptoms. It cannot, overnight, turn him into the Blacker kind of Sicilian. If he marries well though… then perhaps there is hope for one of his sons.

Buzzing in John's pocket.

A text from Kerry:

Bro, tell me the meditation wasn't amazing!?!?!?!?!

John pays for his smokes, plus the gin, then leaves the store. More buzzing. Another message from Kerry:

Also,

There might be something going down tonight
At Corey and Rick's
If you're down
Not sure
Will update you
Peace

Another message:

Also,
le Kyle says hi
Lol

More buzzing. A text from Corey:

Johnny Boy
Park session tonight
???
We never smoked that spliff
At the party I mean
Lemme know bro
Peace

John knows better than to respond to any of the messages right away. Determined to pursue his current mood to its bottom, he heads down the block to the 10th Avenue Safeway where he buys a batch of deli chicken wings and potato wedges that he knows he's earned. They'll carry him over into the next phase of his evening, and he won't have to pay for them again until morning.

Wary of interactions at the house, he devours the food in the parking lot, then smokes again, getting his sticky fingers all over his cigarette and lighter. The gin rests beside him in a paper bag, and he ventures a swig.

Several aghast, pear-shaped Boomers limp-scurry past him to the seats of their SUVs, so as to all the quicker reach the seats of their living rooms. John is still too young, vigorous, and spiritual for any of their RRSP opinions to apply to him, and they know better than to challenge him in any conceivable way.

Barely later: John foreskin lies curled up in the corner of his bed, well into the second trimester of post-masturbatory nihilism. With pressed palms, he draws a soothing, inhuman chill from the wall. Dead quiet, the house speaks to him, and he feels all of it.

They must all be at Corey's.

Fuck 'em.

It is now, with the moonlight cutting through the curtains, and the knowledge that more gin awaits, that a few more facts of life make themselves perfectly plain:

Life is struggle, a person's struggle to do right by the energy bestowed upon them. What isn't exerted upwards through physical toil and passionate speech must be excreted downwards through ejaculation and defecation. What this means for women, John hasn't yet figured, but he knows that menstruation is part of the equation.

What's more, no amount of upward exertion, not since the onset of puberty, has been sufficient to completely alleviate the need for ejaculation. And forgoing ejaculation means fire through the anus and other untold aberrations. It is a futile battle, and true celibacy a myth. Sloth is sin. Rightly so. But so is masturbation. Polygamy, taboo. And nine months of gestation is a long time. Besides, the world already has far too many people.

Meanwhile, through these energetic comings and goings within the body, there form certain inlets and tide pools that distill and circulate of their own accord. John knows, for instance, that his temples are where he keeps the songs that never cease playing, and the songs that start playing out of nowhere, providing timely commentary on the precarity of his waking life. He's always known this, but somehow he forgot it for a very long time.

Until tonight…

And John knows he's been holding back. All his life. Holding back for a day that will never come.

From across the room, the exercise bike scorns him.

He knows he should mount it.

Mount it now.

That's what Sa'ad le Kyle would have me do.

It's like the Center has been part of le Kyle's plan all along.

To clean my head out.

Or…

 Or is it the Universe that's doing everything?

If I am to meet le Kyle's challenge…

If I am to finally correct my colonialist's hairline…

Then I must…

I must summon the courage.

To let it all go.

To empty myself.

Into the black hole.

15

Heinous & Veiny

2022

"Why do you want me to hurt you?"

John Foreskin struts with the confidence of a man who has recently joined the local gym, with the smug knowing of a man on his third week of Finasteride, with the murderous intent of a man who has not vaped in two days, with the catholic shame of a man who insisted upon himself this very morning.

Now that he is getting in some serious workouts, and sweating more from physical exertion than beta-male anxiety, heinous and veiny erections have begun to appear at all hours. John Foreskin is in beast mode, plain and simple, and all young and fertile females ought to be on high alert.

John knows the woman's period is the time for the man to rest and consolidate his energies, the time for the desires of both parties to be denied, and to grow as a result of that denial. He knows full moons play a part, too. He knows moreover how various acts prohibited by the Bible can get in the way of all this (he can think of four in particular), and he just committed one upon himself this morning as the winter sun shone through the bedroom window onto his troglodyte inner thighs. There was been no glory in the act. Only a kind of wrong heat.

John's FTLIJGF—who is a fully autonomous being unto herself—has gone out for the day, leaving John to stave off nihilism through either diversion or the active pursuit of goals, at least until his classes start at 4:30. He barely bothers getting dressed and then leaves his apartment heaven hell-bent on being overly caffeinated in the PM, where PM does not stand for premenstrual even though the levels of caffeination he now intends can easily aggravate his digestion to the point of rectal bleeding. He's somehow rationalized spending on Starbucks or Coco milk tea despite having a full pot of coffee at home, almost as if he wants to retest the hypothesis that consumerism is a viable remedy to his adulting-under-capitalism malaise.

The front doors of his building open directly onto High Road, the outdoor shopping plaza at Marine Drive Skytrain station: T&T Grocery, Tim Hortons,

Starbucks, cinema, Shoppers Drugmart, liquor store with adjoining Irish pub, etc. John heads for Coco milk on the other side of Marine Drive. The cold wind purifies his crevices.

In the shadows cast by the liquor store, downtrodden white supremacists smoke cigarettes and indulge in the mood prescribed by certain rock songs of the early 2000s.

This is how you remind me of what I really am, at least one of the skulkers thinks as he exhales against a Universe that has forsaken him.

In Vancouver, the proximity of a soup kitchen or liquor store all but guarantees such a gathering. John's old neighbourhood in Burnaby had both, and on his way to and from the local Starbucks at the Highgate shopping plaza he would often walk by the sharing circle, complete with beers, a guitar player, at least one fentanyl dealer, and true stories of heroic victimhood.

A Chinese family, bundled uniformly in $1,500 Canada Goose Parkas, enters High Road from Cambie. From behind their N95 face masks, their smiles make the argument that there's no reason on Earth not to be happy. As they pass the liquor store, two opposing forces collide: glass-half-full industriousness and nihilist self-pity. A few of the downtrodden white supremacists squirm. The family laughs and then gain another victory by not looking at John when John looks at them.

As John passes the skulkers, he remembers Jordan Peterson's first rule for life and squares his shoulders. He avoids eye contact, telling himself that he is more like the Chinese family than the grimy whites. And yet he knows how close he's been to permanently adopting their posture, how close he is now to not affording his Vancouver high-rise apartment, and it occurs to him, not for the first time, that his low socio-economic status is incommensurate with his highborn dignity (practically Elven).

According to the paradigm of John's YouTube homepage, what he and the skulkers have in common is a lack of any long-term goals, goals that would motivate intermediary actions, actions that would trigger dopaminergic release without necessarily providing immediate, sedating gratification, goals that would vanquish nihilism by instilling single-minded purpose into every waking moment.

I need to work more on my business.

Expand my client base.

Update my website.

GOOD BOY ALCHEMY

Coco is crowded like always. John's the only legally-colourless person as well as the only person not wearing a face mask.

As he nears the front of the line, he feels the prick of eyes boring holes into the back of his head. He widens his stance and engages the deepest muscles of his glutes to reinforce his aura against molestation. But he doesn't find the courage to actually look behind.

Gymnastics for strengthening the sinews of the soul…
Plato was right.

John's mind flashes back to a friend doing squats in the living room at West 14th.

He orders an original milk tea, 50% sugar, no pearls or other nonsense then steps aside to reassume his chad stance. When he finally dares a look around the café, nobody is looking at him. They're all busy on their phones.

Why do I let them hurt me?

Then John remembers.

The gay boy…
Who called me out…

Tom was precocious. A true man-boy. When he first came to St. Marguerite d'Youville Elementary, he referred to his former school as "a hole." Nobody in grade six spoke like that. Plus he already knew that he

195

was gay, and he knew what that was going to mean for him in this world.

"Why do you want me to hurt you?" Tom asked him. They'd just finished their crossing-guard shift. It was Tom's first week at the school, yet he had already put his finger on one of John's formulas. John's class-mates of six years had never called him out on it, and John had convinced himself that only the Universe knew.

"Why do you want me to hurt you?"

"What?"

"I said would you like a bag for this, sir."

John Foreskin receives his order, unsheathes the piece of shit paper straw, and stabs it into his milk tea right then and there. He exits Coco, into the blustering out-doors, and heads straight back to High Road and his apartment heaven.

A man around John's age is waiting at the intersec-tion. Well-dressed, taller, with brown hair and a mous-tache that feels put on. He could easily be Tom, John thinks, all grown up. The light changes and they cross together.

As John crosses through High Road, the downtrod-den white supremacists scoff at the decadence of his $6 milk tea, which he cradles in both hands like a child proud of his toy. He enters his building, holding the door open for the same man who crossed with him at the intersection. They wait at the elevators together. The man enters first and leans against the back mirror, right in the middle so that John has to stand closer to the door. The doors close and the elevator begins to move.

Why the fuck didn't you move to the side? And now what? You're just going to stare at the back of my head the whole ride up?

"That's right, John. Let me hurt you."

John freezes.

"You know the drill," the man drawls. "Store it on the left side, with the rest of it. And then act like it didn't hurt at all. Hasn't that always been the way, John?"

I'm imagining it. There's no way…

"But they always notice that you haven't bitten back, don't they? That you never even show your teeth." The man chuckles. "So then what? Are they supposed to pity you, John? Should they fear your revenge?"

This can't be real.

"For all those years…What on earth was the point? Unless…unless you were afraid of what would happen if you didn't? Unless you felt like you couldn't actually defend yourself, even if you tried? Or maybe…Yes, that must be it. You felt you were already broken. Too broken to bother."

Shut the fuck up and die!

You're imagining this!

"I've hit the nail on the head, haven't I, John? You thought the one wound you most wanted to hide would stand out if it weren't surrounded by others. So you let them hurt you. Isn't that why, John?"

John's eyes suddenly dart to the buttons. Only the 26th floor has been pushed.

What the fuck.

"But where has that gotten you?" the man drawls on. "Where are you now? And how many of those slights do you still carry, forward down the path? Toward the day of ultimate revenge? And when, exactly, will that day arrive, John? Do you have any idea?"

John clears his throat. His heart wells up, and he can feel his mouth pouting, bound shut by what feels like a thousand stitches.

"And how much lighter are the burdens of your school friends now, all grown up, the same age as you? They haven't been playing the same game you have. How heavy do you feel now because of the choice you made?"

I did what I —

"To survive? Oh, John. Do you really think that's what you needed to do—to survive? Wait. Did you actually think you were being clever? Then how is it the little gay boy saw right through you?"

Floor 26.

"John? Can you answer any of my questions?"

John gets out and turns left, then a right and he's at his door. He grips his keys in his pocket, ready to use them as a weapon. But then he hears the jingle of another set and spins around. The man is entering the apartment across the hall. He turns, gives John a firm nod, then closes the door.

John splashes water on his face then looks at his reflection in the mirror. In four hours, he will present himself at a private academy in the posh neighbourhood of Kerrisdale. His greasy hair will be conditioned, his scruffy face shaven, his shirt tucked in, his shoes correct. And he will have all the answers, and the energy to ask questions. And he will not take shit from any of his students. He will appear professional and worth every hourly dollar he's paid to be the adult in the room.

16

Cycles

2012

Two weeks have passed since John, Kerry, and le Kyle first meditated together in the house on Balaclava Street.

Cafés. Aimless walks. Always the sun. The impetus to give more and the helplessness against sin. Then there are the knowing glances between John, Kerry, and le Kyle. All three have kept on going to the Center and something has developed between them now. In himself, John recognizes a new vulnerability, a proximity to ancient emotions that now threaten to surface.

The next meditation session takes place on an unseasonably hot Wednesday[22] when all twenty-something Vancouverite indolents hate the sun, or else, find-

---

[22] See: Climate Change

ing fault with the concrete, forgive the sun and thank the trees. Since they grew up being told they were special, it doesn't make sense that daily life could be this difficult, unless it is life's fault and not theirs. It takes only five minutes out of doors for the hyperglycaemic to break their no-Starbucks vows, while on crowded busses more than five years old, it is no longer possible to feel gratitude for life or love for one's neighbour.

Le Kyle hasn't been posting up in the backyard where the house and the giant oak provide shade to smoke and reckon; they've somehow evaded John for days. But here they are now, sitting right next to Kerry on the hardwood floor of the meditation room, with only a pair of sweating iced americanos to separate their taut millennial thighs.

"This meditation—the Method—teaches us that humans have *no* soul. No true individuality as we usually conceive of it. Not everyone is ready to hear this though."

Is that supposed to make us feel special?

He's saying the exact same shit as yesterday, and the day before.

Dudek slaps the side of his thigh, jolting John back to attention. "No *me*-ness, yes? But we make one for ourselves, don't we? By telling ourselves a story of *who we are, what we've done,* what others have done to us…"

John knows that if he stood up right now and walked out, he'd be winning—over Dudek, over Adam, over the entire *Center*. He could walk out without saying a word (They'd think he was just going to the bathroom.) and he'd be out the door without anyone seeing him. And he'd have no reason to step foot on Balaclava Street again.

But then…

But then le Kyle and Kerry would think he'd given up, that he was *afraid* of looking inside of himself, or that he didn't have the *grit* to stick it out. And then they'd have the Center between them. And they'd make that their reason for closing him out. John Foreskin recrosses his legs and straightens his spine.

The meditation starts much like the previous session but with a different type of death. Not a fissure this time, but a car crash, and then the family members at the funeral, and then rising up to the Universe.

When it's time to open his eyes and throw everything into the black hole, John gives himself over to the succession of memories that rise up and exit him. Sometimes it feels like they come up from his stomach, through his throat, and out of his mouth. Other times it feels like they are squeezed out of his forehead like a tube of toothpaste.

John finally remembers Amina, the little Indian girl . Her father owned the Lotus Café and always addressed Little John Foreskin as *"boss."* Amina's favourite song was *The Sign* by Ace of Base. And it was a point of pride for her to have a favourite song just as it was a shame for John not to, nor to even know which bands he liked, or whether he was a *skater,* a *headbanger,* or a *rapper.* Amina was only a year ahead of John in school, but she had a favourite song and already knew that she was a skater, and she even wore a chain that attached her velcro wallet with a peace sign to the belt loop of her baggy jeans. John hated wearing jeans and didn't even own a wallet. But from then on he wanted one, and from then on he resolved to retain songs within his head, mainly in the upper-right temple. Not only would this allow him to pull a favourite song down on demand, but it would also ensure that he never lost face in music class by singing the wrong words, be- cause when Marcel had sung the wrong words every- one laughed, and Marcel's face had turned red even though Madame Paquette said he'd been singing *pas- sionnément* and scolded the rest of the class. But it didn't matter because it was still a reason to gang up on Marcel. And so Little John Foreskin was given one more reason to keep even more inside of his head.

By the time the session finishes, they've gone through three full 'life cycles', and John has remembered many new things, long-lost things pulled out from the dark corners of his mind.

"The more cycles we complete, the more new things will come up. The important thing is: continue throwing away."

"How did I know if it's working?" asks one of the Boomers.

"And what if nothing comes up?" says another.

"Or what if the same things keep coming up?" says le Kyle.

"That's okay, brother," Dudek says, fighting back a sigh. "That is actually good thing. Just keep throwing away."

John pictures a slightly younger Dudek being offered the same reassurances. *Just keep throwing away.*

"There are layers and layers. Like onion. And more deeply something has affected us, the more times we must throw it away."

The house is dead quiet when le Kyle, Kerry, and John finally leave that night.

"Where are they?" whispers le Kyle, trying not to let the door slam.

"The helpers?" says John. "I think they meditate up-stairs or something after the sessions have ended."

"Yeah. Or something," says le Kyle, nudging Kerry.

"Maybe they're just tired?" says Kerry. "Ever think of that?"

"Look," says John. "There's a light on upstairs.

"You guys have heard the chanting, right?" says le Kyle.

"Those are upper-level students," says Kerry. "Gimme one of those smokes, Johnny boy."

"How long is level 1 supposed to take again?"

"No sure," says John. "But I met a guy who's been in it for like eight months now. This Boomer dude."

"Level 2 is eyes closed. That's about all I know."

"By the way guys," says Kerry, "I think I'm close to finding my root."

"How can you tell?" says John.

"And isn't that a Level 2 thing? Dudek and Adam have barely mentioned it."

"Just a feeling I'm getting," says Kerry, misty-eyed, and then, as if adding a vital point, "As things begin to unravel."

John rolls his eyes.

So you're quoting Adam now?

"I'm honestly bored half the time. I mean, things *come up,*" *says* le Kyle with air quotes, "but I'm mostly just chilling."

"Isn't your head full of thoughts though?" says John.

"Not really."

"Pizza, you guys?" says Kerry. "I'm starving"

"I'm down," says John.

"You're always down, Foreskin."

"John's the most go with the flow guy I know."

In the early hours of the morning, John lies in bed, staring at the ceiling. A few swigs of gin have set the mood, and he's found that tenderness in his heart that lies somewhere between gratitude and utter despair. And then, like so many nights before, the ceiling disappears, and he's sure he can see the starry sky, and then, beyond the stars, the darkness, distant and immediate, the abyss that is never surprised by his return.

◆

It was not planned. It was not agreed upon. It just so happened. John Foreskin kept going to the Center.

His days there come and go, with more and more cycles completed each time, with more and more of his forgotten life revealed to him. And he allows it all to surface. And the more he goes, the more he thinks about his *root*, the root he was promised he would find, if he keeps on digging, if he keeps on throwing his memories into the black hole.

The other buzzword in the house on Balaclava is *falseness*. "Because when you've died and become a ghost floating alone in the emptiness of space, and everyone you've ever known has died a thousand years prior…"

Well that's when John can finally see…the *falseness* of his ideas.

"Useless illusions," Dudek is fond of saying.

"A weird, fucked-up psychological experiment," le Kyle called it. "All we're doing is staring at a black circle taped to the wall."

Le Kyle was right. And that's still all they're doing. But he keeps coming, and so do John and Kerry. And the more John focuses on that little black hole taped to the wall, the more he notices how little focus he's capable of. And he's reminded of his father, how he used to talk to himself in the car.

A gazillion inanities are constantly rushing up, buzzing around. And in the moments when John truly feels like he's taken the reins, and is *seeing* the black hole in front of him, his face contorts to an ugly grimace, and the tendons in his neck tighten, and his jaw and chin tuck in and downward as his breathing turns to long rushes out of the nose, like a bull about to charge. And then, a kind of gagging begins, as dank air rises and exits through his mouth.

Unaired grievances.

The thought arose last week, from the depths, and John Foreskin did not question it. It was *the Method* revealing things to him, he thought.

And it's in these moments, when he's silenced all the chatter, that John can feel how absurdly constricted his chest is. And then, on cue, he remembers le Kyle's words, uttered on that sunny day in the backyard, with something like admiration, for the man with the shallow chest. "He was a warrior, and that is the stamp of a warrior."

The silencing of John's buzzing head is always accompanied by these contortions. Yet none of the others ever seems to notice. And none of them has complained of any similar symptoms.

Before almost every meditation session there is a lecture, given by either Dudek or Adam, sometimes both, and John soaks up every word, even though the same ideas keep getting repeated, again and again, day after day.

And every session begins with the same words: "This is a real situation. Let's truly die." And John truly does, or thinks he does, then judges himself for doubting that he has, then tries again, only to curse himself for trying, instead of simply surrendering.

And after every visit to the Center, he rewards himself with something iced, typically a latte. Cigarettes feel that much better following sessions, too. And then, once the sun has set, literally anything feels permitted because he knows he's at least made a dent, that he's edged just a little bit closer to balancing his account with the Universe.

◆

After the first month of meditation, 1-on-1 sessions are announced to mark the transition from Level 1 to Level 2, and John, Kerry, and le Kyle are among those asked to attend. Some of the Level 1 Boomers have been going to the Center for several months already, but if they resent how fast the three Millennials have cruised through the level, they aren't showing it.

"What remains?"
"Nothing remains."
Dudek sighs. "Let's try again."

John's insides are reeling, but he nods, and they start over...

"And now, all that remains of your lived life is being sucked into black hole...

0 to 10 years old, suuuukkkkkk!

10 to 20 years old, suuuuuuukkk!

20 to now, suuuuuuukkkkkkk!

And now, even ghost shell is sucked into the black hole, SUUUUUUUUUKKKKK!

What remains?"

"The Universe," John replies after the briefest hesitation.

Why did I think before answering?

"Okay," says Dudek, almost as a question. "Let's take a break."

Fuck

"Relax outside. We try again."

John patrols the perimeter of the house on Balaclava Street, smoking, and wrestling with the indomitable impulse to think abstractly. He stares at knots in the planks lining the side of the house, minute pebbles on the ground, single blades of grass, trying to see the world in front of him and condemning every thought that pops into his head.

I've spent a month staring at a little black circle, and I still can't focus for shit.

How did Kerry and le Kyle pass already?

The way they're practically skipping through the house…

Those fuckers.

He rounds the corner of the house, selecting the picnic table as his next point of focus, but his mind jumps to him walking right out the back gate, down the laneway, all the way home to West 14th.

Why did those fuckers have to pass?

The next thing he knows, he's re-entered the house and is taking off his shoes.

"And now, all of your lived life, from 1000 years ago, all that has been stuck inside of you. Only you know about it. Only you have it. That entire life story exists only within the three-quarter pound hunk of meat you call brain. Entire story of man called John. Now, all of it is being sucked into the black hole…

Suuuuuukkkk

Suuuuuuukkkkkkkk"

Dudek's voice deepens.

"Suuuuuukkkkkkk

Suuuukkkkkkk

Suuuckkkkkk

Sukkkkk."

His voice grows louder, more powerful, as he begins to exert himself.

What does he want from me?

The entire house must be able to hear him.

"Your childhood. School days. Friends. Family. Birthday parties. Vacations. Summer activities. Graduation.

Suukk

Suukk

Sukkk

Suuuuuuk

University. Girlfriends. Jobs. Problems with parents.

Suukk

Suukk

Sukkk

Suuuuuuk

Everything up until the moment of your death…

Suukk

Suukk

Suukk

Suukk!"

As Dudek's voice grows stronger and stronger, so does a tugging feeling in John's gut.

What is he doing to me?

"SUK!

SUK!

SUK!

SAHHHH....

And now even the empty ghost shell is sucked into the black hole...

SUK!" Dudek thunders.

And as he empties his lungs, John feels the familiar weight of his gut rise an inch and then...

...disappear.

"Take a moment to meditate in this state."

John loses himself in...

Silence

Some time later, the question arrives:

"What only remains?"

"The Universe remains." Before John knows it, he's answered.

"Yes."

From the left side of his body, John coughs, and something escapes him. A weight. Ancient. He rises then, as if powered by a spring, and exits the room. The next several minutes blur by.

He finds himself sitting against a tree in a nearby forest, his left leg splayed in front of him, his right tucked under his buttocks. His hands rest on the ground, palms up. And his mind would be thoughtless, except that he knows he doesn't want the tears streaming down his face to stop.

He wipes his nose with his sleeve. His inside has emptied, finally. He felt it happen. Something invisible, and gelatinous—it unravelled itself and exited his left leg, into his left lung, then out his mouth. It happened when he spoke his answer.

The Universe.

He spoke without thinking, and it was like opening a floodgate.

From my left side.

I keep everything bottled up there.

That's all Dudek wanted from me.

Through a glaze of tears, he sees the resplendent forest. He blinks, wiping his eyes, as a large oak tree comes into focus. As he regards it, he feels himself regarded. And then, to his astonishment, they become one, and it feels as if he is looking at himself, like he is both the tree and the body known as John, and the space between.

I've actually died.

It is the only notion his blank mind can conjure. And then, for an indeterminate space of time, there is only awareness.

Birds sing from the trees, their voices passing right through him. Patches of light and shadow dance on the forest floor between his legs. Absent thought, all is splendour.

But as quickly as it came, it begins to subside, and John is aware of an abstracting away, a grasping, to make the experience *his own*. And also, a despair, deep and hollow. The gap of a severed tethering. It was never meant to be a permanent move, to this place. And he already wants to go home.

And so he finds it again.

Thy will be done.

That familiar, grounding weight.

My story so far on the earth.

That's what they'd tell me.

…what they want me to give up.

The faint hankering for a cigarette spells the end of the little treat that Dudek and Adam promised would come, *"From the Universe, when you're ready."*

John rises, more or less himself again, and stumbles out of the forest into a park he doesn't recognize.

I can't be that far from the Center, can I?

Smiling, he lets the thought go. His mind turns to Dudek, then to Kerry and le Kyle. He almost wants to cry again. But people and dogs are in the field and what he needs now isn't more unravelling. It's solidity. Sleep. Heavy food. And that cigarette.

He stops at a sushi joint on 10th Avenue and orders his usual, a sixteen-piece combo for $7.50. Unheard of in Ottawa.

As he waits for his order, he observes the gradual busying of his blankened mind. Notions coast past, voices, images, and with each passing one the urge to latch on grows stronger.

He finally gives in, indulging the observation that he is currently unconcerned about the state of his hair. And then it is already too late. For this is succeeded by an image of how his hair likely appears, and, in turn, by the unassailable mandate to locate a reflective surface. By the time his order is ready, he is anxious to leave the restaurant.

Once home, he grabs a beer from the fridge, telling himself that

    a. He's earned it,
       and
    b. The 'rightful' owner can surely spare it

Alone in his basement sanctuary, he eats his sushi too quickly, feeding unaired grievances, it occurs to him, more than his body. The chatter grows louder, crowding back in, and he takes a swig from the green glass bottle, as much to celebrate what's happened, as to mourn its end.

17

Anatman

2022

Per Buddhist doctrine, there is no John Foreskin, per se.

John catches a glimpse of his un-posing self in the bathroom mirror and sees the face of his father.

The same smugness.

The same grim countenance, stiff with the chronic resolve to never relinquish whatever it is that men hold onto for dear life.

Whatever changes the boy's innocent sparkle to the man's weary glint.

Whatever sees emotional continence outlast intestinal continence.

Whatever sees men strive against the Universe's prorogative the one and only entropy—the force that would see every human's precious sense of self disintegrate into oblivion.

John goes back to bed, careful not to wake the pokémon beside him. Infantilizing pet names aside, he closes his eyes.

Awareness

Thought.
Images.
Verbal thought, thinking in words.
Silent awareness vs verbal thought.
The songs that play without John's consent or contrivance.
The songs that are only melodies.
Deliberate verbal thought vs automatic songs.
Mental BGM, if one will.
If one wills it, can one vanquish them?
From the temples.
Since childhood.
From choices made.
Supervillain hairlines.
Deliberate choices.

Awareness

Facial tension.
Bodily awareness.

Mental image of the bedroom.

I am here.

Eyes open: the bedroom.

Eyes closed: the bedroom.

Bodily awareness.

Awareness identifying itself with the body.

Awareness.

Verbal thought.

Bodily sensations.

Awareness disassociating from the body.

Awareness letting go of the bedroom.

Awareness letting go of the body.

A rush of the heart.

Vacuum.

Oblivion.

Life.

Source.

Spirit.

The Universe.

Awareness

Awareness reaching back for the sensations of the body.

Facial tension.

Awareness identifying with the body.

Verbal thought.

"I."

Morning.

John Foreskin regards himself in the bathroom mirror that holds him to account. Every millimetre more of jawline represents a week since the last time he masturbated; every millimetre less of forehead, a month. And John doesn't vape anymore. That is huge. But he still abuses caffeine.

"Stupid fucking Caucasians and your daily Starbucks."

Think super thick Hong Kong accent.

Think, JC, John's former landlord.

Think intergenerational wealth amassed by forgoing such $6 luxuries long enough to become one of Vancouver's landlord class.

Think John needing any excuse to leave his damp basement hovel first thing in the morning, just so he can interact with humans other than Mitch the obese, balding, alcoholic, Trump-worshipping biblical scholar.

Finasteride seems to be working, too. Slowly. But working. New sprouts have begun to appear, indicating that John's hairline could actually regain some ground in its war against the mass of adult-male-forehead sagesse.

Half a centimetre.

Dark.

Less Scandinavian.

More Sicilian.

As he pours his morning coffee, he reflects on the sugar content of bubble tea, and then on the suffocating silence of inter-male elevator rides.

Maybe this is why grown men become the way they are.

All stiff and gruff.

They are standing up for something!

So that they don't fall...

For literally anything.

As the caffeine begins to work, so do John's higher faculties, allowing him to formulate the following regarding the Patriarchy's toxicity:

Premise 1: Virtually all men suffer from emotional constipation.

Premise 2: Reticence does empathic violence to oneself, others, and the female Yin.

Premise 3: Virtually all men are committing patriarchal violence against the very fabric of the Universe.

~

Conclusion: Every thorny-tongued word a man utters that is not from an open heart, that does not surrender his self to the sharing circle, harms himself, others, and the Universe.

Soft snoring from the bedroom. The pokémon still slumbers. John plops down in his captain's chair and engages his monitors.

Stop chasing what you think will make you happy

says Allan Watts in the thumbnail of yet another wisdom-mongering YouTube video on the front page of John's daily excuse not to pursue any one long-term goal in particular.

John is fairly certain that the Jordan B. Peterson video beside it,

Advice to Young Men

will expound something to the diametric contrary.

John recrosses his legs, and then sips his morning coffee, all the while tugging compulsively at the newborn French Bulldog that is his flaccid, uncircumcised penis.

18

Confessions

2015

"Dismiss sensory perceptions.

Dismiss the image of the room, the belief, sustained by the image, that *you* now sit in the room you remember.

Dismiss the somatic impressions that sustain your belief in being, as an embodied creature.

Dismiss the notion that *you* are now *seeing,* with *your* eyes, that these sense organs are what now enable you to *perceive* the darkness.

There are no eyes.

Darkness is perceiving darkness.

Shed the mask that you feel trapped behind.

Darkness dwells within darkness.

Darkness dwells within itself.

There *is* a knowing.

Rest here, in the knowing…

Simply rest…

And now, open your eyes."

Twenty pairs of eyes crack open, and a moment later the curtains follow.

"Well done, everyone."

The entire audience sits cross-legged in the large meditation room on the second floor of the Center on Balaclava St.

John, Kerry, and le Kyle sit in the second row. Dmitry is here, too, sitting right next to le Kyle. He started coming about six months ago and has since caught up to the others in the levels of the Method. They have their own clique at 4474 West 14th and spend all their free time at the Center.

The speaker—tall, thin, possibly mid-fifties—is visiting from The Main Center in Budapest. As she speaks, she moves her hands gracefully, and her green eyes, tired but inwardly bright, appear to rest on each audience member in turn.

"You are not here to save face, everyone, yes? You are here to *lose* all of your faces. By now, I think this should be very clear, even to those of you in Level 1." The speaker squints, as if straining to see the back of the room, and then frowns.

"We are each of us on our own path. We are all of us on the same path, yes?" She begins to pace.

"And none of us can claim superiority over anyone else." She stops, resting her gaze on Dudek, Adam, and Hyemin until all three lower their heads.

For days leading up to the visit, Adam and Dudek had the upper-level students clean every millimetre of the Center as part of their 'action meditation,' and neither held back in their role as taskmaster. The impending arrival of the guest speaker brought out an urgency in them that John and the others had never seen before. After a room was finally pronounced clean, Hyemin would walk through it, spreading incense and mumbling a prayer. "Keep dying" is all the helpers said whenever any of the students betrayed resentment for the work. Since the arrival of the guest, however, the only words uttered from the helpers' mouths have been "Yes, sister."

"Students and helpers alike. Isn't that right?" She resumes her pacing. "We are all on this path together. And I'm here today, visiting from the Main Center, to provide you all with some reassurance, and convey to you some of the energy that the Method has afforded me."

John glances at Kerry, sitting upright, an innocence in her eyes.

"Are any of you here familiar with Descartes's first principle? Descartes famously stated, *cogito ergo sum*. I think?" She extends her hand.

"Therefore, I am," most of the audience answers.

"Very good. Or, if you like, *Je pense, donc je suis*." Her green eyes sparkle as she enunciates the French. "But I want to tell you today, brothers and sisters, that this is commonly misunderstood, especially in so-called *spiritual* circles." The speaker grins, then strikes a pose, popping out her hip and clasping a hand over her chin. "Actually, I think Descartes was quite a deep guy."

Chuckles from the back of the room.

John shifts on his cushion.

Level 1 fucks. Why were they even allowed to attend?

Into the black hole.

Be grateful to the method.

"After all, there *could* be a demon deceiving us, as Descartes said. Can we really know beyond all doubt that the world and our bodies exist as we perceive them? Tricky, no? But more importantly, what did Descartes mean when he advocated meditating *a priori*, independent of prior experience?" The woman's gaze settles on John, and they swim in each other's eyes until she finally pulls away.

"Je veux dire…When we close our eyes, do we not continue assuming all kinds of things about our circumstances? And are these assumptions not sustained by the continuous feed of sensory impressions we receive? Even with our eyes closed?

"So how can we appreciate Descartes' endpoint if we cannot first join him at his starting place? What sense of *I* might each of us discover if we joined Descartes there, a *priori*, where *logos* has separated itself even from the echoes of sensory perception?"

Frowning, the speaker pauses, and gives a long nod, as if looking at the audience from above a pair of reading glasses.

"The Tao Te Ching calls it Darkness. *Darkness within darkness. The beginning of all wisdom.* So what I want to convey today is that you *can* exist without believing that you exist. And believe me when I tell you that you *believe* you exist." She chuckles to herself, bringing some of the audience with her. "That's a kind of…what do you say in English? A tongue-squeeze?"

"Tongue twister."

"Ah yes! A tongue twister. Thank you, Brother Adam."

More chuckling.

The speaker has begun to blush.

"You entertain the belief that you exist. And you rarely *cease* entertaining it. The method, as I'm sure you've been told *so* many times now…"

John looks at the speaker's subtle gestures, the way she appears to grasp, pull, and release, to swim as she paces, and, for a split second, he sees thin threads of light extending from her hands to each person sitting on the floor.

"The method is about e*xisting.* Period. It's really that simple." She pauses to drink from a bottle of water. "Curtains please."

Hyemin rises like a spring, and a moment later the room is dark.

"If you close your eyes again now—yes, I bid you—you will notice that the mental picture you've taken of this room is rather…complete. You reside in the room even when your eyes are closed. And you have an idea of where the door is located, who is seated beside you, the sources of light…"

John doesn't dare open his eyes. But the others are thinking the same thing. They've gotten used to hearing the same ideas over and over again. He notices his resistance to the words, his impulse to reject them, to protect himself. But he resists the impulse to resist. He chooses surrender. He chooses faith. In the Method. He chooses to *die.*

"For now, the majority of you are still convinced of certain boundaries, which is fine," the speaker says with a shrug. "Maybe it is the back of your neck? Maybe the face? A mask, yes? You feel yourself stuck behind it. And maybe you feel your arms and legs? Your posture? These sensations, whatever they may be, all prop up the proposition—there's another tongue twister!"

More chuckles.

"They *prop up the proposition* that you exist. There is the proposition that you are here in this room, that yourself and the room are distinct, and that you now, with eyes closed, are experiencing *being here* in this room.

"But to even get close to joining Descartes, we have to first of all separate from the senses. No, we do not *suppress* them. Do not plug your ears or jump in a tank. Nor is it about imagining a different setting, or getting lost in daydreams. We simply have to appreciate that…"

That we can entertain and dismiss…

John's heard it all before. Dudek and Adam began feeding them this line at the start of level 2.

"…propositions separately from our ability to sense our surroundings and the state of our bodies."

The doorbell rings.

A momentary pause.

John keeps his eyes closed.

A door opens, then clicks shut.

"Notice, I don't *deny* us or our bodies. I'm talking about an ability we possess as human beings. In the same way, the exercise of ceasing to believe that we exist is not about arriving at some truth that we don't exist. We are *here*. But, again, our being here has absolutely nothing to do with our *believing* we are here. Our believing we are here is a proposition that *does* take some amount of energy to sustain, even if doing so has become second nature, habitual, we can say."

The speaker pauses as the door clicks open.

John cracks open his eyes to see Adam reentering the room and the speaker producing a small, red pocketbook. The cover of the book is embossed with a golden "D". He shuts his eyes again.

"Reading for you now from the original Handbook of the Method: The immediate reaction of the organism to the contrary proposition, "I do not exist," can be quite jarring. When earnestly entertained, it invariably induces a catharsis, the symptoms of which embarrass the self-possessing adult.

"And then on page forty... With eyes closed, setting aside the imagined room that our four active senses continue to generate is a rather obscure feat that very few individuals venture deliberately outside of a monastery or temple—except, it must be noted, in cases of extreme duress and trauma.

"So you see, my friends, even that simple denial can produce some strange reactions within us, and that is partly why I'm here today, to walk you through that and to reassure you.

"But to really follow our cher ami Descartes down this path, we *do* have to detach from our senses. Certainly, not a skill taught in school. It is a subtle kind of psychology, n'est pas?"

She sounds smug.

Just die.

Stop thinking,

Stop judging!

"Every word that comes from my mouth now and all of the background noises of this house and the street outside reinforce your mental picture of the room you now inhabit.

"And so now again, from page 27 this time: The realm of the rational, as distinct from that of the somatic and emotional, can either be completely possessed by the five senses, or else it can detach itself, and deal purely with the propositional. It is only when one achieves the detached state that one begins to glimpse the primary proposition, that of one's own existence.

"So now, with eyes closed, denying the proposition that you are sitting here, in this room, that *you* are experiencing things, will bring all kinds of tension and resistance to the surface. Sometimes this is because the mind is confusing the denial of this proposition with the death of the body. This is partly because you are losing all of your normal orientation and partly because you are resisting the ego death. You are refusing to die, as I'm sure your helpers have told you a thousand times by now. But even beginning in Level 1 of the Method, all of you sitting here know how important dying is, right?"

A few people murmur.

"It is really the ultimate confession. You are revealing to the Universe everything that you're still holding on to, everything you've claimed as yours, everything you've mistaken as *you*. *All* of that is...how do you say..up for grabs? All of that is up for grabs when you begin to deny the p*rimary proposition.*

"And on that very point, reading now from page 51 of the Handbook of the Method: It is perhaps the central paradox, for it lies at the tender heart of our Universe, that those things which we cannot accept, those things for which we cannot feel gratitude, are the very things we refuse to let go."

Indignation suddenly threatens John's composure. He feels hot all over, and, somehow, accused.

"Very good. Please open your eyes now, and I should like to say thank you all, for your effort this afternoon."

The audience stirs and claps as the speaker offers the slightest of bows. Hyemin rises, and a moment later sunlight pours back into the room.

"And so yes, to the question posed earlier, from—I believe it was—the young lady Kerry. It *is* correct to say it is a kind of death, the most important kind of death, in fact, that one can experience while living on this earth. It will not lead to you *dying,* my friends," the speaker says with the most knowing of smiles. "As in, falling over and never waking up!" She pretends to keel over, then recovers with a laugh. Adam and Dudek join in. The room erupts. Even Hyemin raises a hand to her mouth.

"Rather, it will lead to even greater freedom, and so much more beyond that, which you cannot even begin to imagine." The speaker shares another knowing smile with the helpers. "So now let me leave you all with a little secret, which I don't mind mentioning now because none of you won't get it at first anyways, unless you are already quite a ways along in the Method.

Jesus Christ, kill me now.

The speaker leans forward with her hands on her knees, and lowers her voice as if revealing her schoolyard crush: "Letting go of the proposition that *you* are having this experience is the same as *the Universe* realizing that *it* is having this experience and that it has been the Universe *all along*." She stands upright again, concluding in her normal tone: "And that is why we must confess, brothers and sisters. Confess everything."

◆

The more time John spends at the Center, the more he's convinced that Dudek and Adam perform private, lust-tempering exercises, that the exertions he witnesses around the Center grounds are far from the extent of their daily labours. He counts their curt manner and the robustness of their hairlines as evidence of his theory.

Compared to them, he feels weak. And permissive. He resolves to use his exercise bike more, and do actual pushups on the hardwood floor of his basement sanctuary. And once more he swears off masturbation. Two days later, still disgusted with himself, he swears off Starbucks, cold turkey. A week into his new chad phase, he announces his Starbucks resolution to the others, scolding himself afterwards for craving their audience.

A real chad would just do it.

Near the end of week two, he takes a rare night off from the Center. Pacing the hardwood floor, he looks first at his laptop, then at the exercise bike, then at a stack of his old school books. He picks one up, an old old favourite, and begins flipping through pages. But he's quickly turned off. The convoluted sentences. The airs of the writer. It feels so out of touch and complicated. He opens his closet door. His Swedish red pullover is hanging up. He can't remember the last time he wore it. His style has become somehow more vanilla, and he doesn't give much thought at all to his clothing these days.

Faint chatter drifts in from the backyard. It's too early for the others to be back from the Center. He considers joining whoever's out there for a smoke, but his stomach is still sick from his last one.

I need to quit.

There's a knock at the door.

John opens it. Kerry looks at him, her eyes deadly serious. The next thing he knows, she's closed the door behind her and they're facing each other.

John's heart is racing. But a smile begins to spread across his face as he realizes how he's wearing his nervousness like chainmail armour, an excuse to keep Kerry at a distance.

Kerry's eyes soften, and she breaks eye contact to survey the room. It's the first time anyone from the house has actually been inside. His sanctuary.

"Not exactly what I expected. Cleaner, actually. Do you even use that thing?"

"The Bike? Sure I do."

Kerry looks at John's full-length mirror next, frowning, then at his desk, then back to John. Then she turns, flicks off the light, and moves towards the bed. "Come here."

John follows and sits beside her. They sit there for a long time as the sun goes down outside and the darkness gathers around the glow of John's laptop. The backyard chatter dies down, and John can hear a faint raspiness in Kerry's breathing.

"I came here—" she finally says. "I came here because there's really nowhere else to go."

John's throat dries up.

"But that's actually a good thing," she continues, "because I really don't want this to be personal. And at least you're doing the Method, so I know you'll understand…and be able to throw it away."

"Throw what away?" John asks, his voice breaking.

Kerry pushes him onto his back and perches herself on top, her eyes now fixed on the wall. She sits there motionless for several seconds. Then, ever so slowly, begins rocking her head back and forth. As John's eyes finally adjust to the darkness, he can see the furrow in her brow. He's seen that look before, at the Center.

Is she —

She's practicing Level 1.

The tenderness in his pants suddenly registers, and he looks past her face to where the ceiling should be. But it's gone again. There's only the abyss. And the subtle glow of Kerry's skin.

The tiniest of moans escapes her. John recognizes the sound. They escape him, too, in spite of himself, during the meditation. And their tone always startles him, as if a momentary lapse in vigilance has allowed his true self to cry out for help.

Kerry presses her hands into his shoulders and begins to slowly gyrate her hips. He tries to focus on the darkness, but there's nothing to fix his gaze on.

"It's nothing personal, John."

He dares another look at her eyes. Her bone structure is glowing.

She's ascending.

He scoffs at the thought.

It's my mind.

Or…

Or we're both ascending!

Together!

I'm—

"Keep dying, John," Kerry says.

She senses it, too!

He squeezes his eyes shut, and the darkness rushes in. Filling him. Sickening him. He opens them again.

Kerry is shining, her eyes still fixed on the wall.

John's pants are wet.

Kerry grabs his right arm with one hand, putting her other hand in her pants.

"Keep dying, John."

John Foreskin died a thousand years ago.

The universe is seeing the universe.

He tries to find the ceiling. But he can't. It's gone. He cannot believe it is gone, but he *knows* it isn't there. He *knows* that he is not *seeing* with his eyes. He's feeling infinity. He can feel the bed beneath them, but if he were to look for the floor, he thinks his heart would stop from the shock.

Kerry begins to moan.

John's eyes jump to her face.

Nothing animal.

She's an angel.

The painful tenderness wells up. He squeezes his eyes shut again, but the darkness is too much and he opens them.

I must be dreaming.

Kerry's face changes again. It's her. But it's not her. It's...

It's the Starbucks goddess.

"You've been avoiding me, John. Why? You know you want me." Her long, wavy hair cascades over her breasts. "Come again when you're ready, John. You deserve to drink from me."

John blinks and the image begins to fade.

"I'll be waiting for you, John..."

Kerry moans, cocking back her head. "Keeping dying, John!"

John grabs onto her arms as his back arches, and the two Caucasian millennials die at the same time.

Kerry rises, and John covers himself just as she flicks on the light.

She surveys the room again, as if forming a new opinion, and John rests his gaze on her with no thought for the weight of it.

They both smile.

"What is it?" she asks.

"I lied to you. The other day."

"When?"

"When I told you I hadn't been to Starbucks in over a week? That was a lie. I went on Saturday."

"I see," says Kerry, grinning. "That's quite the fib now, isn't it?"

"I don't know why I lied."

"That's okay, John. You're still a good boy."

19

The Humanity

2022

Keen on meeting his POC UBC[23] compatriot, Simon "The Wang" Wang, John Foreskin attempts to determine whether a certain park near his interracial cohabitation sky mansion permits BBQing. He finds himself using the chat help on the City of Vancouver website...

Karen

Online

You sent

Hi. I'm wondering if there are picnic tables in Queen Elizabeth Park for BBQing. Do you know? Thanks.

Karen sent

Hi! My name is Karen.

Designated picnic sites do require a permit. Reservations are made online: vancouver.ca/parks-recreation-culture/picnics.

---

[23] Person of Colour , University of British Columbia

Here are the terms and conditions regarding picnics in the park: vancouver.ca/parks-recreation-culture/picnic-site-terms-and-conditions.

Here are the guidelines: vancouver.ca/parks-recreation-culture/picnic-policies-and-guidelines

BBQs are permitted as long as the fire danger warning for BC is not at extreme.

Please check with the province: www2.gov.bc.ca/gov/content/safety/wildfire-status/wildfire-situation/fire-danger

From the list of available designated picnic sites, I do not see anything listed for QE Park.

You sent

Designated requires a reservation.

Non-designated does not.

Correct?

I'm just speaking of picnic tables, not necessarily designated ones.

Does that make sense?

Karen sent

Designated locations require a permit.

Picnic tables in general outside of these locations would be 1st come 1st serve.

You sent

Thank you

This I know.

I'm just asking about the presence of non-designated tables.

In QE park.

Karen sent

Picnic tables in general outside of these locations would be 1st come 1st serve.

To clarify...outside of the ones listed as designated.

You sent

You've stated that there are no designated tables in QE Park.

Have you stated anything regarding the presence of non-designated tables?

Karen sent

There are ONLY designated picnic sites that require permits. All other picnic tables are 1st come 1st serve.

You sent

Saying there are only designated tables, and then saying there are 'other tables' doesn't make sense. Am I crazy?

Karen sent

Let me clarify again. On the picnic site link provided above, it lists locations for designated picnic sites that require a permit. You cannot use those sites unless you have a permit.

Everything outside of those designated sites is 1st come 1st serve.

You sent

Yes. That's clear. Thank you. Have you answered this question: "Do you know whether there are non-designated 'picnic tables' (wooden tables) located in QE park?" ?

I'm wondering about the existence of such tables in the park.

Karen sent

Non-designated to me would mean unmarked or unassigned for a specific purpose. Ones that are marked would be designated.

You sent

That sounds reasonable.

Do such non-designated tables exist in QE Park, as far as you know?

Karen sent

I personally do not know if there are picnic tables in QE Park.

You sent

I see. Thank you for your patience.

Karen sent

There are no designated picnic sites there. However, there could be picnic benches placed around the grounds for people to use at their leisure. That is what I mean by undesignated.

You sent

Any picnic table that does exist there must be non-designated, since it isn't listed, right? And it's okay to have a picnic on such tables, including with a BBQ set, right?

Karen sent

We don't sign unregulated picnic tables. People are free to use them. Please review the picnic guidelines link also provided above.

You sent

Right. I see. We are free to use them, but you're not sure if any exist in QE Park. I understand. Thanks for your patience, and have a great Friday.

Karen sent

I don't know if there are picnic tables at QE.

You sent

At this point, I must conclude that you are an AI, not a human. No offence.

Is this correct?

Karen sent

No that is not correct.

You sent

Oh... I think we've had a breakdown of communication then. I was sincerely trying to express myself clearly though... I apologize.

Karen sent

No apology necessary. It may be easier to explain verbally. You can always call our information line to speak to someone.

You sent

Hmm. Okay. Well thanks for your time and patience.

Karen sent

No problem. Happy to have been of assistance.

John Foreskin closes his internet browser, swivels to face the balcony window, and then speculates on the likelihood of this City of Vancouver civil servant possessing a master's degree.

20

Omnia Mea Mecum Porto

2022

I knew, and then I didn't know, and then I knew again.
I knew, and then I forgot. Then I remembered.
I knew. I forgot. I remembered.
I knew. Then I forgot what I knew. Then I remembered.

John Foreskin brushes the back of his tongue until he gags from his root chakra, thereby achieving his second petite mort of the morning. He spits the residual sins down the drain and then rinses his toothbrush. Teary-eyed, he looks into the bathroom mirror that holds him to account.

Sheer villainy.

The colonialist's mirror secret.

The wicked temples of cunning.

The white man's conceit.

In medieval depictions of the devil, the horns symbolize nothing other than the receding temples of the man who has eaten ravenously from the Tree of Knowledge. So clear to those who bother to think about it.

Disgustingly sweet morning milk tea notwithstanding, John Foreskin is unbearably sober. And yet, John Foreskin is sick with theories, surely.

He emerges from the bathroom sometime later, more certain than he's ever been at any previous point in his existence about nothing at all.

His would-be productive daylight hours proceed with him comparing the contours of his forehead to those of Ryan Gosling's circa *Lala Land*. He'll reach sundown as accomplished as any man ever has been: with a grande Starbucks drink—light ice, adjusted sugar level, unspecified lactose-free milk option. Untouchable in his sky mansion, he'll speculate vaguely about how it is that others seem to be better than he at adulting under capitalism, before eventually taking yet another stab at the immovable mass that is his foreheaded past.

Drained from his mirror session, he approaches the bedroom window and looks up at the evening sky, who he's perpetually at odds with for all of the things he's kept hold of, seemingly for dear life.

The sky.

Living.

Infinite.

His life.

A being turned inward onto itself.

> Fully given to the voices
> In denial of his choices

And he can't help but crack a smile. He forgets, for such long stretches at a time. But tonight he's remembered to…consult the ledger.

> Brow backed up with old accounts.
> Hating god with every ounce.

Now, if Twitch or YouTube doesn't seduce him, he might to work out some old kinks, and bring himself that much closer to the world he forsook all those years ago

when he chose,

consciously,

as perhaps only a child can,

to screw up his eyes

and stop looking at the sky,

to stop really seeing it.

When he chose

to live inside his mind

because

that seemed easier than coming to terms with the

world

and his less than lofty station in it.

John Foreskin collapses onto the bed and brings to mind his father the only way he knows how: by feeling his father's face on top of his.

A mask.

A mien.

To wear.

Or to shirk.

But perhaps,

Never to shed.

Never completely.

To know his father is to be his father.

To bring to mind anyone now is to wear their face.

John rises and takes another sip of his grande iced latte. Then he closes his eyes again to face the darkness, to suspend the picture of reality otherwise maintained.

He proceeds as he's been taught, by denying it all.
Or is it letting go?
When the chatter finally stops,
And his faces grow
Furious.
It has always been this way.

Paying dues to closeheld burdens

Only the temple chatter
(levity afforded by his iced mocha)
was keeping the despair at bay.
But it's always there,
waiting for those moments
of neither productivity nor escapism
(John's dichotomization of adult waking hours),
waiting for John to let it all go.

Omnia Mea Mecum Porto.
All that is mine I carry with me.

And John must believe that he can let it all go.
He must believe that humans possess that power.

21

The Root

2016

The winter months at 4474 West 14th see a retreat en masse to private quarters. Safe spaces. Warm spaces, too, as the noble millennial savages pay no gas bill and rely on electric space heaters for at least three months of the year. People walk around the house in winter jackets and most of the girls wear Ugg boots.

As the sun relents, many begin to fatten up and all anyone who is a mammal wants to do is hibernate and have what little vigour is left at the end of each day sucked or humped out of them. It is commonly felt that to sleep without the body heat of another human is just about the worst fate a person in the first world can endure. Hookups between tenants who barely speak during warmer months are not uncommon, and territorial tensions rise whenever too many couples happen to be living in the house at the same time.

Officially, there are no double rooms (something about bylaws and human trafficking), but non-tenants stay over all the time, while couples comprising two house tenants often end up spending most of their time in just one room. The influx of outside partners makes for longer bathroom wait times, greater variation in odour, and more 'nothing about this is awkward' mornings in the kitchen—mornings when girls don oversized hoodies over bare legs, and boys, if the relationship is still fresh, resort to ostentatious ball scratching and possessive kisses on the cheek. It feels the good kind of sticky to know that at any given moment couples are getting it on or maybe just binging a show. And John can always duck downstairs and lock his door when it all becomes too much. His real refuge from all the humanity isn't his bedroom though. It's the Center.

"Are you a real person? Let that question sink in." Adam stands surveying the ranks, twelve or so seated on the hardwood, in levels 3 and 4, most wrapped in thin blue blankets.

Fuck he's arrogant.

Shut the fuck up and die!

John sits in the front row, eyes fixed on the floor.

"What does it *mean* to be a real person?"

Why does he talk down to us like that?

Shut the fuck up and die!

He's been meditating for longer!

It's nothing cruel.

"Are there real people in your life right now? If so, who might they be? And how would you even know?"

John pictures Segan whom he hasn't thought of in years. She certainly *felt* real. She *kept* it real. But they lost touch, just like so many others from the past. There are faces of people who lived with him at 4474, but he can't match them with names. And now he hardly speaks to any of the new tenants; he couldn't even tell you who last moved in, or when that was. And what would he even have to say? *"Have you found your root yet?"*

"Well? Are you? A real person?"

"No," says Kerry, from her seat against the wall.

Of course.

Shut the fuck up and die!

"No," a few others mumble, Dmitry's voice rising obnoxiously above the others'.

"As long as the answer remains no, we must continue to die. We die—"

And we throw away the falseness.

"—and we throw away the falseness." Adam begins to pace the front of the room. "In Level 1, we threw away our lived lives, our remembered thoughts. Floating in the Universe as a ghost, we saw that all of our conceptions existed only within ourselves, and were of no use to us. We alone were holding onto them. We alone knew the story we'd told ourselves about who we were on the earth all those years ago. And when even the empty ghost shell was sucked into the black hole, we saw that only the pure, empty Universe remained. The living Universe. Our true self."

He should be a pastor.

"In Level 2, we went even deeper. We found that the heavier parts of the human mind comprise our attachments to the people we've known in our lives. Thus, we threw away pictures of our relationships with others, pictures of ourselves, and again, our very selves. Every one that we uncovered. When the Universe Giant came down and pulled out the last remaining human mind like a glob of jelly from your gaping chest, you were emptied, and you saw that there *is* no human mind, no inside and outside. That was the gift waiting for you at the end of Level 2. No inside of you and outside of you. Everything is just…"

"The Universe," a dozen voices chime in.

"Now, some of you have already found your *root*. And some of you *think* you have. But if you're not sure, then you probably haven't."

John looks over at Kerry, head bowed, back perfectly flush with the wall. She was the first to find hers, followed closely by Dmitry, and then le Kyle. But they were told not to discuss it with anyone except the helpers. That was around the time the four of them stopped hanging out as much as a group, around the time Kerry started wearing shawls and having less to say about things. Of the eight students at the Center in level 3, John is the only one who still hasn't found his root.

"For those of you who *have* found your root, congratulations. You ought to keep revisiting it when we throw away our lives because the more your root unravels the more everything else begins to fall away."

And that's when heaven begins.

"And that's when heaven begins."

John shivers as a draft penetrates his blanket cocoon.

Is heaven warmer than this fucking room?

He straightens his back as Adam passes.

Shut the fuck up and die!

"But still. Still! When we close our eyes, die, and go to the Universe, we cannot help but feel as if we are still here, inside this room, inside these bodies. Isn't that right, brothers and sisters? In other words, we have not yet ceased narrating our lives. We have not yet killed the false self. And so we are playing roles. Even now, some of you meditating are just playing a role, a role that you don't even know you're stuck in."

And what a shame that is.

"What a shame that is."

Silence from the group.

Same fucking thing every fucking time.

Shut the fuck up and die!

John looks over at Dmitry, bundled in his blanket, and le Kyle, who looks to be dozing off. They've both changed so much, and John's witnessed the transformation.

"But that's okay. Why?"

We have the Method.

"Because we have the Method. As long as we have the Method, we have hope. What about those people outside the Center? Those who have never even encountered the Method? Think of how trapped they are, hopelessly trapped, without even knowing it. As difficult as this path has been, brothers and sisters, and I know it has not been easy, at least here, we *have* the Method."

"Thank you to the Method," someone murmurs, and the rest of the group follows suit.

"In Level 3, we continue to throw away pictures of our lived life as in Levels 1 and 2, and we begin to also discard this very body, even down to the cells. For that is where all of our habits are stored.

"Finally, we also let go of our ancestors who are living inside of us, who want us to believe that their way is the correct way. But none of them were alive to meet the Method, were they? So they don't know any better. Just imagine how happy they will be when you release them into heaven."

Adam dims the lights, and people shift on their cushions. John catches Kerry's eye, and they exchange a nod.

"I am grateful to the Method," Adam begins.

And everybody joins him, "of removing all that is false in me that must be truly thrown away."

Le Kyle perks up. Kerry stands and moves her cushion to join the group in the center of the room.

"I am grateful to the Method of removing all that is false in me that must be truly thrown away."

By the end of the tenth recitation, some people are shouting. Others barely mumble. Again, people shift on their cushions, and John can feel the resolve setting in.

"By now you've noticed that most students don't finish Level 2. They come and go, some staying longer than others, but most end up leaving. So if you're here now, give yourself a pat on the back. This is your chance. Don't let go of it." Adam pauses.

John sees the trick he could be playing, the trick he probably is playing. But he's already come so far, already discovered so much.

He takes them through a quick review of Level 1. As always, he assures them that it is perfectly normal to find brand-new memories that haven't come up in previous sessions.

Then he takes them through Level 2. This time the Universe Giant rips open their mouths and reaches down to pull out their *human mind* through the throat.

"There is no human mind. There is no inside and outside. There is only the living Universe."

John fends off a wave of self-consciousness as his teeth begin to chatter. It began in Level 2, but the helpers have assured him that it's just his body's reaction to the Method, to the falseness exiting. If any of the others have noticed it, they haven't said a thing.

"Now, myself sitting here, this self that still claims to exist, the Universe Giant comes down, scoops me up and brings me *millions* of lightyears away to a remote corner of the Universe. He throws me down onto a giant chopping board! It's the size of a football field! And beside it is a giant vat of acid. Then, he chops off my arms!" Adam's voice grows deeper, more hollow:

"JAT!

JAT!

My legs!

JAT!

JAT!

And finally my head!

JAT!"

John's anxiety soars as Adam's voice seems to stab at the boundaries of his mind.

But I'm not on a chopping board in space! I'm right here! In this room! Trapped in my body!

Shut the fuck up and die!

"Next, he takes the head and plucks out both eyes.

BUK!

BUK!

He places them on the chopping board and begins chopping them with his knife.

JAT!

JAT!

JAT!

JAT!

The eyes that I use to judge everything that I see. The eyes that deceive me. Can I really see anything that is true with these eyes that are rotten to the core?

JAT!

JAT!

JAT!"

Again and again, Adam's voice stabs at John's mind, causing John to hate him and love him in turn, as more and more is broken loose and released.

"JAT!

JAT!

JAT!

JAT!"

Just stand up and leave.

Kill him. Then leave.

Shut the fuck up and die!

How ungrateful are you?

Adam is a real person. He's completed the Method!

His voice can drive out the falseness in you!

But only if you surrender!

Just keep dying!

"JAT!

JAT!

JAT!

JAT!

JAT!

"Why are you holding on? Do you want to be trapped inside this hunk of meat after you die? Free yourself!"

John winces, trying to refocus.

"JAT!

JAT!

JAT!

JAT!

JAT!

JAT!

JAT!

JAT!

JAT!"

The tiniest of whimpers escapes his throat, and Adam's voice relents slightly.

"JAT!

JAT!

JAT!

JAT!"

I died!

Thank you!

Thank you to the Method!

"The Universe Giant throws the chopped-up parts into the vat of acid.

Ttsssssssssssss!"

Adam's voice fills the room, passing through John, and clearing all the dust stirred up by the chanting.

"Ttsssssssssssss!"

Thank you, Universe.

"Now the escalator appears, leading to the grinder and the vat of acid below. One by one, the Universe Giant places each of your ancestors on the escalator and sends them up to the grinder. Every ancestor, going all the way back to the dawn of humankind is placed on and sent to the grinder before dropping down into the vat of acid.

DRRR.

DRRR.

DRRR.

Ttsssssssssssss!

DRRR.

DRRR.

DRRR.

Ttsssssssssssss!"

John can feel himself beginning to let go.

"DRRR.

DRRR.

DRRR.

Ttsssssssssssss!"

The room disappears.

"DRRR.

DRRR.

DRRR.

Ttsssssssssssss!"

He loses his orientation within his body.

Where is my mind?

Have I died?

"The last of your ancestors! They're all disappearing into the acid!

DRRR.

DRRR.

DRRR.

Ttssssssssssss!"

He feels on the verge of letting go completely, but at the last second, he recoils back inside of himself. The room falls silent.

He's sure that Adam knows.

No!

Shut the fuck up and die!

Following Adam's instructions, they begin surveying their lives and throwing all of the memories they find into the Universe Grinder along with the very self possessing each memory.

John's mind goes quickly back to his childhood home on Uplands Drive and the weight he'd carried there from their previous home on Rochester.

Then Dalhousie Street and his old daycare.

And then a new memory…

The senior playroom. It's brightly lit. John and his playmates, their hands in the sand bin. Sitting at the craft table. White glue bottles. Cat and Mouse under the parachute. The young ladies who are not John's mother. They shepherd all the children, calling them *guys and gals.*

John sees his friend, a sullen boy whose returns from the washroom can always be felt.

Now John needs to go.

He's in the hallway now. Little boots and lunch boxes spill out from cubby holes stuffed with snowsuits. The baby room is at the end of the hall, and then on the left, the bathroom.

Now John is sitting on the toilet. He never closes the stall door. Nobody does.

A frigid wave of recollection.

The daycare custodian.

He enters with his mop and bucket, whistling.

He sees John.

John knew him.

What was his name?

But his mind cannot reach there. Nor can John make out the man's face.

They regard each other, and the custodian's move to put down the mop does not register as strange.

Then he's in the stall.

It is John's fault for not closing the door. And now what is happening is his fault, too. The pain pours out of the man, into John. For John to make his own. One hand is choking John's neck while the other does everything else.

John can't breathe.

And then it is over.

"Ya." John understands that his parents won't love him anymore if they find out.

"Ya." John knows how to keep a secret.

22

Drama

2022

"There was once a lifeform that developed language and abstract symbolic thought, plausibly in this causal order, but perhaps not...

By abstract symbolic thought, we do not merely mean this lifeform possessed the faculty of recall, such that an echo of past sensory impression could spring to mind, intentionally or otherwise, to occupy the conscious awareness of the being and draw at least some attention away from their present, concrete circumstances, if you even will.

Putting aside the reasonable conjecture that even perception of present surroundings entails interpretation, categorization, evaluation, prioritization—and thus abstraction—we shall pursue the present point by clarifying that by abstract symbolic thought, we mean that, in addition to terms such as "wood" or "food" that could plausibly at a given time refer to some object presently sensed, this lifeform's mentation featured concepts such as "past" and "future," "love" and "goodness."

Their faculties of language and thought led this lifeform in all kinds of interesting directions. For one thing, they eventually came to delineate between forces under their control and forces beyond their control. Please allow me to explain.

This lifeform was conscious of willing certain actions. On the other hand, they were also conscious of performing certain actions *without* having willed them, or indeed, despite having willed *not* to perform them *and* despite being unencumbered and uncoerced by any other member of their species or any other organism in their physical surroundings.

Now let us clarify a few things:

1. When any lifeform delineates between forces (or wills) within their control and beyond, they may or may not, in so doing, be delineating between forces originating within *themselves* and forces originating *outside* themselves. For a lifeform that understands itself to be *simple*, all opposing forces would be understood to originate from *outside* of the self. Whereas, for a lifeform that understands

itself to be *complex*, opposing forces could be understood to be part of the self.

2.   In a similar vein, the distinction between that which is within the self and that which is outside of the self may or may not be identical—according to a given lifeform's operational paradigm—with the distinction between that which is within the physical body and that which is outside of it.

3.   We may also note at this time that choosing the term "will" over "force" may introduce personal connotations which may or may not be in keeping with our present mode of strictness. Having said that, an appeal to parsimony does not, prima facie, justify a preference for the impersonal (or mechanistic) over the personal.

From the preceding few points, it follows that we cannot assume this lifeform, in distinguishing between wills under their control and wills beyond their control, was *definitely or definitely not* referring to

(1) wills either inside or outside of *their selves*

(2) wills either inside or outside of their physical bodies

(3) wills understood to be personal in nature

If you are still with me, then next, please imagine a vast, dark sea. Looking upon this sea, we can barely discern a thing, yet vaguely, gradually, we ascertain its complexity. That is, we see that it is not wholly one. Disparate parts clash, some combining, some consuming, some insidious, some repellant. And in a moment of rash projection, we ascribe the term "will" to each distinct part of this sea.

Now imagine that one of these *wills* attains the divine gift (or evolutionary accident) of self-consciousness. Let this newly awakened will illuminate so that a single point of light appears in the vast, shrouded sea. Now among the sea of opposing wills, there is one that *knows its own will.*

The complexity of the sea does not entail that it be physical, mental, spiritual, or any other category of substance we may posit. Yet we know there is multiplicity. And, in so far as there is tension and opposition, we can say there is drama.

With this image of the sea in mind, let's return to the lifeform.

Imagine that, with its self-awareness and abstract thought, this lifeform proceeded to differentiate between the different wills that it perceived in opposition to its own, naming them so that they might be easily referred to, even when not presently acting upon them.

Thus, to refer to instances when one's own will is taken over by a sudden will to attack, this lifeform came up with a concept approximating "rage" or "bloodlust." And to account for times when they felt empowered, not of their own accord, but rather by some external will, to do something necessary but dangerous, they came up with a concept approximating "courage." And they even used this concept to help account for times when this will did *not* act upon them, and they were left quite alone to witness its absence and the misfortunes that befell them as a result. It was understood to be something *other* than them, this *courage*, if only because *they* were aware of both its presence and its absence.

Not all of these wills were paid equal regard. Courage was among the favourites. Death, for its part, opposed the lifeform's conscious will to endure indefinitely, just as sleep opposed their will to remain lucid.

As there was no suggestion that these wills did not have the same approximate countenance as the lifeform, you may not be surprised to hear that they eventually came to personify them. Their existence was unquestionable, so then why would this lifeform think that these wills should not also possess a personality akin to their own, with things they found pleasing and things that vexed them? In light of this point, we may consider the third of the above-enumerated ambiguities to be resolved.

Having personified the wills in this way, eventually, this lifeform began seeking out an audience with some of them, in the hopes that a particular individual or an entire nation might wield a will external to its own—or if not wield one, then be visited or possessed by one, at a time deemed favourable.

It was in this way, ever so gradually, that these wills came to be regarded as something like gods. And the lifeform began to have some say in their relationships with these gods, or so they believed, with some people and peoples favouring certain gods over others.

And now you may be imagining scantily clad savages dancing around a fire, chanting to some "imagined" deity.

But of course, such condescension would entail a few unjustified assumptions:

1. The delineation between the internal and the external of the so-called physical body (the second of the above-enumerated ambiguities—which has yet to be resolved with regard to this lifeform).

2. Default credulity towards perceptions apprehended by the organism's external senses, and simultaneous incredulity towards any 'non-sense'

perceptions apprehended *inside* the body or *inside* the mind.

3. The assumption that this lifeform never actually succeeded with any reliability at currying the favour of their gods.

As unsatisfactory as the dark sea metaphor may have been, it does manage to avoid these pitfalls.

So, at present, we are not in a position to claim with certainty anything about the *substance* of the willscape.

Jumping ahead somewhat, some members of this life form eventually came to posit a single will of an entirely different order, both compared to them and to the multiplicity of wills they had come to regard as deities. For one thing, this *arch will* was presumed omnipotent. And this arch will, it was understood, had *willed* not only them, but the entire willscape, i.e. it was the one will that willed all lesser wills into willing.

Thus, something like monotheism arose. So instead of a god of courage being directly beseeched so that one might *wield* or *be possessed by* courage, the one god was beseeched so that one might be *granted* courage. But since this shift happened contemporaneously across disparate cultures, drama arose when two monotheistic cultures did not believe in the same one god, which may or may not be to say they did not *share the same understanding* of the very *same* arch will.

When wars broke out, they were frequently justified by the will of the one god, and victory was attributed to the will and reality of the victors' god and to the un-reality of the losers', or else to the loser's belief in mul-tiple gods). Almost invariably, the losers would adopt belief in the winners' god. In this way, over time, monotheism of one strain or another spread until pre-cious few pockets of the old paradigm remained.

In the old paradigm, the wills-turned-gods were understood as autonomous and *other.* Moreover, none of them was considered strictly bad or evil; rather, it was simply understood as inevitable that one's own will, or the collective will of a people, would encounter opposition within the willscape.

The new paradigm, however, cemented a new di-chotomy: all fortunate encounters with wills other than one's own were understood as *blessings* originating from the one god; all unfortunate encounters were un-derstood as evil originating from *within (?!)* a given member of the lifeform.

As you can see, this new dichotomy entailed anoth-er: the inside vs outside of each member of the lifeform. So in this way, the first of our three original ambiguities is resolved, i.e. at this point in the lifeform's development, they understood that they were contending with multiple wills dwelling *within* themselves as well as a single will external.

You could say that the simplification of the *external* willscape, from poly- to mono-, coincided with the complexification of each member of this lifeform (Hence my use of 'member' in the last several paragraphs instead of the problematic *in*dividual).

In this way, the drama was largely internalized, such that one engaged in perpetual struggle with oneself— with one's own wills—while maintaining an external relationship with the one god. Members of this lifeform understood themselves to be at the mercy of the one god's will, while their *own* wills were to be interrogated, suppressed, repented, and surrendered."

John Foreskin is roused by the distinct sound of vaccine-hesitant construction workers earning an honest day's living without necessarily harbouring sentiments approximating racism or misogyny.

Their tanned vigour
is his pale shame
is their contemptuous gaze
is his failure to meet theirs
as he sets out on his stern

but loose-bowelled

pre-screen

morning walk

in honour of his organism's

dopamine and serotonin systems,

mainstays of a paradigm

introduced and maintained

by the algorithm of John Foreskin's

YouTube front page.

The shoulders of the men he encounters are invariably
broader than his own.

23

Shut the Fuck Up & Die

2017

Darkness dwells within darkness.
Darkness dwells within itself.
There is a knowing.
But is it the true darkness, or a false one?
How many worlds have I created
since turning inward, away from Truth?

~Handbook of the Method, p.76

1. Myself who does not brag about the Method
2. Myself who isn't grateful to the D
3. Myself who does not repent
4. Myself who feels lust
5. Myself who cares what others think
6. Myself who doesn't have faith in the D

7. Myself who is not grateful for the Method
8. Myself who does not do action meditation
9. Myself who is lazy
10. Myself who knows only myself
11. Myself who has turned his back on the world
12. Myself who craves knowledge
13. Myself who keeps others in my heart
14. Myself who is not grateful to my brothers and sisters
15. Myself whose words hurt others
16. Myself who insulates himself from the world
17. Myself who thinks he is the center of the world
18. Myself who feels envy
19. Myself who collects samples of the world
20. Myself who leeches off others
21. Myself who always puts himself first
22. Myself who is ambitious
23. Myself who blames others
24. Myself who is cunning
25. Myself who tries to possess others
26. Myself who seeks approval
27. Myself who is incomplete
28. Myself who is a slave to the body
29. Myself who doesn't die
30. Myself who has enemies
31. Myself who does not blame myself
32. Myself who meditates only for myself
33. Myself who pities myself
34. Myself who has family
35. Myself who blames the Universe
36. Myself who is gluttonous

37. Myself who does not believe in others
38. Myself who blames the D
39. Myself who says "I alone can do it"
40. Myself who seeks pity from others
41. Myself who is incapable of telling the truth
42. Myself who always thinks of the future
43. Myself who cannot let go
44. Myself who blames the world
45. Myself who craves an audience
46. My self who tries to save face
47. Myself who cannot see myself
48. Myself who has money
49. Myself who is waiting for the afterlife
50. Myself who harbours anger towards the D

"Shut the fuck up and die." John Foreskin marches against the wind, all hunched shoulders and vehement muttering. Pine cones are kicked for being unworthy, and fault is found in small children. Overhead, dark clouds gather.

Three days ago, the Level 4 students were given small manila envelopes. Each contained a slip of thin paper, a light pastel red, no larger than a receipt. Filling both sides was a typed list of fifty selves to be discarded one thousand times each in preparation for the Final Education. Dudek said the envelopes arrived in the mail from Budapest, and the weight of that one word set everyone to their task. *Budapest.* The Main Center. The birthplace of the Method.

John was home in bed that day. He couldn't bring himself to go anywhere, not even Starbucks. And definitely not the Center. The helpers had warned them against focusing too much on their roots. It hadn't meant anything to John at first because he hadn't found his. But once he had, he glimpsed why they might say that, the morbidity it could engender.

Nevertheless, for John, the Method became about digging up his root. What else inside of him could have driven him to this point? Why else would the Universe have set him on this path, to meet Dudek, and then visit the Center? What else could justify the hours he'd spent, the days, weeks, and months, year after year, in the two-storey house on Balaclava Street?

Dmitry slipped the paper under his door after he had pretended to be asleep. Dmitry, the one person he almost told.

They were sitting in the backyard around sunset one day, and John could feel Dmitry's heart. It was always the same when they sat together smoking, often with nothing much to say to one another. And he suddenly felt like he could tell him. Like Dmitry could bear the weight. He was about to, but he ended up just thanking him. And then they hugged. And Dmitry never asked why.

When John finally dragged himself out of bed, it was to check the bags under his eyes. The more he focused on his root, the more sunken they became. Not all the time. There were patches of light. And he *felt* lighter, more himself. But he couldn't just leave it alone. He had to keep on digging, looking in the place where, for so many years, he'd been too afraid.

He got up to check his eyes. They'd felt tired all morning. And that's when he saw the envelope. And then for the first time in years, he thought about Dr. Varma's report, what she'd said, what she'd known at the time, and where it might be now amongst the piles of books and papers that lined the walls of his room.

That score she'd given me. I made such a big deal of it. But I didn't even know. I didn't know what she didn't know. And how could she have? I was still —

How about now then? What kind of shape am I in?

Surely better.

The Method.

It's shown me my root.

I'm getting to the bottom of things

And reversing the Basic Formula as well.

But then why...

Why am I so fucking tired all the time?

"Shut the fuck up and die."

Universe, please kill me.

John bumps into someone on the sidewalk but presses on without looking back. West 10th is bustling as people rush to beat the storm.

"Shut the fuck up and die."

His greasy hair is matted backwards, accentuating his supervillain temples and revealing everything he's stolen from the world. He was so focused on discarding the fifty selves that he forgot to check his mirror before leaving.

The freedom of not knowing. The feat of abstraction required to even pose the question: What do others see, when they look at me?

A sudden pang in his left foot causes him to hop then slow his pace. An elderly boomer speed-walks by, his neon spandex a sex crime. He meets John's eyes. His smile fades.

John keeps going, hoping to walk off the kink.

Did I pull something?

For a solid three weeks, he was using flat-footed squatting to subdue his RMJs[24]. Then, once he received the red slip, he realized the Universe's plan, how he'd already been killing selves 4, 25, 27, and 28. He was en-

---

[24] Rambunctious Morning Johnsons

joying that feeling, of being filled to the brim. He felt closer to understanding Adam and Dudek, too, how they could live in that house, with Hyemin, and never try anything. But he fell off that wagon last night, sometime after his third shot of gin, and now, as he veers onto the uphill stretch of Alma, both forehead and foreskin are in tatters from overuse.

Binge and purge, Bitch.

"Shut the fuck up and die."

The sun streaks through a sudden break in the clouds, her touch mirking him as if none of the meditation he's done over the past five years has counted for anything, as if he's no closer to balancing his accounts.

Nemesis.

Fuck this hill.

"Shut the fuck up and die!"

Universe, please kill me.

Myself who blames the world.

Meanwhile, his light-iced grande almond milk latte isn't doing its usual trick, and he's barely feeling his third cigarette of the day. On today of all days.

Just get to the Center.

And be grateful.

For the Method.

Passing one of his usual sushi places, he glimpses his reflection.

Sheer villainy.

He immediately ruffles his hair to obscure his temples.

Fucking Christ.

Universe, please kill me.

Myself who cares what others think.

He pushes up the hill, vision tunnelled, and the clouds slowly close. He does not see the autumn leaves swirling in the wind. He does not hear the children at play in the nearby schoolyard. He already knows his destination, as well as how to get there. Routine affords him his abstraction. For five years now it has run a jagged line of fifteen blocks between his group home on West 14th and the Center on Balaclava Street. A few coffee shops and takeout places along the way fuel him. Even the academy where he teaches part-time sits only a few blocks off his main path. Vancouver, the city, remains foreign. When he does venture into other neighbourhoods, it's to distribute pamphlets.

John approaches the Center from the back laneway just as the first drops of rain begin to fall. Entering the yard, he sees Le Kyle and Dmitry performing action meditation in the vegetable garden.

"Thank you for your effort," John mumbles.

"Thank you for your effort," they call back, not bothering to turn around.

A group of lower-level students are seated at the picnic table, some younger than John. They look up as he passes, hungry for some sign that they're on the right path.

Self #1. I'm supposed to brag.

Tell them how swell life has become, all thanks to the Method.

He recalls how he looked up to Dudek, right from the start, like the big brother he never had. Adam and Hyemin, too. How he thought they were in heaven. That's what they sold him, the way they conducted themselves.

Now I'm supposed to be?

Kerry said it. They're not gods.

So then what are they? What have I become?

"Shut the fuck up and die. Shut the fuck up and die," he rasps hoarse, and the students lower their heads.

They'll be leaving soon anyways. Tonight is not for them.

Plopping down in the kitchen, he finally shuts his eyes. And he finds it there, waiting for him. The darkness. It wraps itself around him like a blanket. He breathes in deeply and his shoulders relax.

Thank you.

It's always there waiting for him. Reminding him why he keeps coming back. At home, too, in bed. He looks for it, and it's always there.

"Hello, brother."

Kerry is standing in the hall, dressed in her usual flowing robes. "Thank you for your effort."

From his seat, John offers a slight bow. "Thank you for your effort."

Kerry glides past and begins filling the kettle. John jumps up and buries his head in the fridge.

"There's never any food these days."

"What you see in there is for tonight," says Kerry, her tone maternal. "Don't touch it." She clicks on the gas stove and then sits down at the island.

"Looks like a storm outside."

"Yes," says Kerry, eyes on her hands.

"Have you seen Dudek? Or Adam?"

"Yes."

Is that all you can say?

Shut the fuck up and die!

Universe, kill myself who is not grateful to my brothers and sisters!

"Are you okay, John? You seem…agitated today."

"I'm—I'm fine."

"You're pale. And you're sweating. More than usual."

You're not a helper!

Shut the fuck up and die!

She doesn't know!

"Might be the caffeine. Plus I was up late last night. You know. The fifty selves. And tonight."

"Yes. Thank you for your effort, John." She lowers her head.

John feels himself relax, feels Kerry's goodwill.

She's so beautiful. She looks...

Universe, please kill me.

Myself who —

"She's not a god."

John jumps out of his skin.

Kerry doesn't budge.

Le Kyle strides in, his shirt wet with sweat, his nipples poised for jousting.

"W-what?"

"She's not a god," he repeats, looking at John, then at Kerry. "You always look like you worship her."

Kerry finally looks up. "Thank you for your effort, brother."

Le Kyle smiles curtly. "Thank you for your effort."

Dmitry walks in. "I found another shovel in the shed, Kylie. And the seeds from last week." He's smiling, at all of them.

"In a second," le Kyle snaps.

The kettle starts to whistle.

Kerry and le Kyle lock eyes.

Dmitry looks at John and shrugs.

"Dmitry!" Adam enters the Kitchen. "What are you doing inside?"

"Sorry. I was just—"

"Your sorry is worthless to me," he yells over the whistle of the kettle. "Do you not see that?"

Kerry hurries to the stove, her composure all but shattered.

"If you're not dying right now then you might as well not attend tonight. I'm not kidding. Nobody here has time for anything else."

Dmitry walks out, head down.

"Have you finished with the toilets, Kerry? Our guests will be arriving soon."

"Not yet, Adam."

"When you're done, Dudek needs you in the office."

Kerry bows. "Thank you."

"And le Kyle, when you're done in the garden, please find Hyemin. You'll be helping her with the food."

"Got it."

"John, can I talk to you for a second?"

John follows Adam into the hallway and then to the small meditation room.

"Wait here."

"Okay." John clenches his jaw to stop the chattering of his teeth. Through the window, he can see the garden. The rain's really starting to come down and some of the lower-level students are helping Dmitry gather up the tools and supplies. He turns on the light and approaches the poster on the wall. The stick man, his giant head weighed down. He inhales, correcting his posture.

When will that stop being me?

"Okay, John?"

Adam and Dudek are standing in the doorway.

"Huh? Yeah, I'm fine."

Adam gestures to the floor, and the three of them sit.

"Your cheque bounced today," says Dudek.

"What?"

"Are you having financial troubles, John?"

"No. I mean, I don't know how that happened. The academy paid me on Monday."

"You know what tonight means, don't you, John?"

"Yes. I do."

"And you know it isn't about the money."

"I know."

"You can attend," says Adam, "but I need that cheque from you by tomorrow. Is that clear?"

"Okay. Yes. Thank you."

"Alright, then."

They rise.

"Are you ready for tonight then?" says Adam, his tone lighter.

"I'm ready."

Dmitry rests his hand on John's shoulder. "And you're grateful, John? To Method?"

"Yes. I'm grateful."

"That's good, John. We need gratitude…to keep going."

Adam stops in the doorway and turns around.

"The Method is the only way. You know that, don't you, John?"

"I know."

"It will all be over soon," says Dudek.

"I know."

"So, are you ready to meet Damond?"

"I'm ready."

24

The Owner of the Universe

2017

"The Avatar Damond."

"Who is the owner of the Universe?"

"The Avatar Damond."

1 AM. Hour five of the Final Education. Over forty Level 4 students pack the dimly lit room on the second floor of the house on Balaclava Street, while outside, rain pours down in sheets.

Most of the students drove up with their helpers from Portland and Seattle, and some from as far as Sacramento. One flew in from Montreal and another three from the Toronto Center. John Foreskin sits among the Vancouverites. Students from the other centers are likewise clustered together. Even during the banquet, there was little intermingling, as it was clear that, though all followed the same method, unique vibes had developed at each Center. Only the Quebecois man seemed oblivious to the mood and John felt bad about not reciprocating his friendship

"Who is the owner of the Universe?"

"The Avatar Damond."

"The Universe kills me.

TANG

TANG

TANG

TANG

TANG."

The helpers, all male, stand at the front, taking turns on them. John Foreskin feels himself molested. Molested then cleansed, over and over, as their voices penetrate him, stirring up everything inside.

"The Universe kills me.

TANG

TANG

TANG

TANG

TANG.

Prayer. Five times."

"I am grateful to the Method of removing all that is false in me that must be truly thrown away. I am grateful..."

Hyemin sits cross-legged, off to the side, along with five other women, one from each of the local centers. Eyes closed, they sway gently from side to side.

On the front wall, a projector shows a live feed from Budapest. But it is only a silhouette, the silhouette of the man they have learned to call Damond.

"Who is the owner of the Universe?"

"The Avatar Damond."

The question is posed, like a challenge, and answered in perfect unison, shouted by many, at the row of helpers, and the motionless silhouette above them.

"Who is the owner of the Universe?"

"The Avatar Damond," John rasps, his throat sore.

The Avatar Damond.

It was true as soon as John heard it. Naturally. The person who created the Method, the only way for humans to find the Universe mind, must be the Universe itself. Only somebody with the pure Universe mind could clear the path. But they needed time, time before they could accept it. So for long, the answer to so many of their questions had remained: The Universe.

"What remains after you've died and disappeared?"

"The Universe."

"What sees and knows that you've died?"

"The Universe."

But now John knows. Now he has faith. Damond sees and knows. Damond is the Universe, the Universe come to save the Universe. The universe come to awaken itself. Clean. Pure. And John Foreskin and everyone else can become that way, too. *Complete,* they call it. They can all become complete. But only with Damond's help. Only with the Method.

Hour six. Still no stop to the rain. The helpers stand at the front, bellowing from depths that shake John to his core. If only he'd surrender. He clenches his jaw to stop the chattering, then cracks open his eyes to have a look around the dark room. Many lie prostrate. Some kneel, their heads bowed. Still others stand, stomping the floor or pounding their fists against the wall as they wail out their repentance. A few, like Dmitry, sway back and forth, not uttering a sound, hands stretched out to the silhouette on the wall. Every voice sounds hoarse. Nobody has repented enough.

Turning to his left, John sees beads of sweat covering le Kyle's brow. And behind him, Kerry is crying. He knows not to look back or even to rest his attention on her for too long. They are all together here, at the Final Education. Yet they are each here alone. He closes his eyes.

"Who is the owner of the Universe?"

"The Avatar Damond."

"Who is the owner of the Universe?"

"The Avatar Damond."

"Myself sitting here is sucked into the black hole."

"SUK

SUK

SUK

SUK

SUK

SUKKK!"

"It's all my fault!"

Everyone joins in.

"It's all my fault!"

"It's all my fault!"

"It's all my fault!"

"It's all my fault!"

Hour Seven. Still not the slightest movement on the Budapest feed.

It's a test. Of our attachment.

If we want it too much, it will repel him.

Myself who wants it has to die.

Damond, please kill me.

The rain has finally let up, so that in the stillness of the night, the urgency in the helpers' voices sounds more forced. But this is not a thought that John permits himself.

"Look at your pathetic selves. Do you really think you can enter through the gates of heaven with the cunning mind of a snake? Do you not think Damond knows the difference? Do you not think Damond will know when he looks into your eyes?"

"It's all my fault!"

"It's all my fault!"

John cracks open his eyes. The figure on the wall sits still. He's sure he can sense his presence though, here in the room.

Even as a boy, I never felt alone.

Has it been you, all this time?

"Those of you still holding on really need to ask yourselves what you're doing here," says Adam, almost yelling. "Maybe this isn't the place for you."

"It's all my fault!"

"It's all my fault!"

"It's all my fault!"

"Your bodies are poisoned with selfish desires. Your bodies are cancer."

"None of you sitting here has even tried to set free your ancestors," says Philip, the helper from Toronto. "You all cling to them, unable to act for yourselves. Truly pathetic."

"It's all my fault!"

"It's all my fault!"

"It's all my fault!"

"All of you are weak and selfish. Nobody here is honest. Nobody here is clean."

"It's all my fault!"

"It's all my fault!"

"You all love yourselves more than the world. More than the Universe. More than Damond. Nobody here deserves to be saved."

"It's all my fault!"

"It's all my fault!"

"Who is the Universe itself?"

"The Avatar Damond."

"Who is the Universe itself?"

"The Avatar Damond."

"Who is the Universe itself?"

"The Avatar Damond."

Hour eight. John's been in and out of the room a few times now. Bathroom breaks. Smoke breaks in the backyard with students from the other centers. People from all walks of life. He can feel something, something they all share.

The few who've made it through.

All the levels.

"We're close now," an older lady from Portland says. "I can feel it."

"Yes," says Yves, the man from Montreal. "Damond is doing everything. It's out of our hands now."

A young man from Sacramento stands by himself near the back lane, wiping tears from his face. The others don't seem to notice, and John leaves him be. That was him, just an hour ago as it may be again an hour from now.

After each break, John rushes back into the room, fully nicotated and slipping on his socks, his vigour renewed, his faith unshakable.

Hour nine. John begins to feel it. It has been building for hours, and now the air feels poised. Something begins to pull at his gut. His gut, swollen with his most precious treasures. He's never been ready before. But tonight feels different.

Damond is making it different.

If I could only surrender.

I can *only surrender.*

The Universe can only take away what I'm ready to give up.

Damond can only —

Again, the sharp pulling at the whirling mass in his gut. If not for that mass, John senses he would lift off the floor and float up to the ceiling. His legs are past shaking, past numbness. His eyes are beyond open and closed, his mind beyond time, his teeth past chattering. His jaw simply opens and snaps shut again, open and shut like a clockwork viper. He's emptied his lungs a thousand times. But always below, the purple fire of his belly embers, flaring up whenever he feels closest to truly letting go.

Again the universal impetus that would see it all dissolve into the cosmos.

Again John resists, incapable of imagining life without it, unsure that he would continue existing were it to finally leave him.

The room ignites with another round of prayer.

"Whose fault is it?"

"It's all my fault!"

"It's all my fault!"

"Myself who meditates for myself?"

"It's all my fault!"

"It's all my fault!"

"Myself who is not grateful for the Method?"

"It's all my fault!"

"It's all my fault!"

"Myself who thinks I am the center of the world?"

"It's all my fault!"

"It's all my fault!"

"Myself who harbours anger towards the D?"

"It's all my fault!"

"It's all my fault!"

And then, in the next lull, a soft rustling from the Budapest feed, like a throat clearing.

A new urgency fills the room, emanating first from the cries of the helpers, then taken up by the sea of students. And off to the side, a silent, synchronized tantrum, as six bodies sway, and six heads shake violently up and down, side to side.

"Whose fault is it?" a helper bellows.

"It's all my fault!"

"It's all my fault!"

"Myself who has gluttony?"

"It's all my fault!"

"It's all my fault!"

"Myself who has pride?"

"It's all my fault!"

"It's all my fault!"

There is no peace here.

Shut the fuck up and die you stupid fucking piece of worthless shit!

John looks at Hyemin just as her shaking intensifies, her mouth contorting into a grotesque pout.

He squeezes his eyes shut again, ashamed of all his self-possession.

Why can't I surrender?

"The Universe Giant chops my body in half and I'm sucked into the black hole."

"BUK!

SOOOK!

BUK!

SOOOK!"

"It's all my fault!"

"It's all my fault!"

"BUK!

SOOOK!"

"It's all my fault!"

"It's all my fault!"

"BUK

SOOOK!

BUK!

SOOOK!

"All I can do is surrender. All I can do is pray for Damond to take it all away."

John recognizes the voice of Dudek, disarmed, pleading with them.

He leans forward and rejoins the chanting, giving voice to a part of himself that, until now, has been too afraid.

"It's all my fault! Please kill me!"

The purple fire reignites his belly as a thousand minds come alive, all coiled together, all claiming their right to remain where they have for so long slumbered and fed.

"It's all my fault! Please kill me!"

And not from the center of them, but off to the side, John Foreskin feels it, his Original Secret. The mind he received that day in the daycare. And he begins shedding tears, utterly helpless against the permanence of it, and pitying himself, for how little of life he's known on his own.

Myself who pities myself!

Universe, please kill me!

Damond, please take this away!

He continues to pray under his breath. "Damond, please take this away. Damond, please take this away."

It's time to let it go now.

The Universe pulls at his gut.

The mass resists.

"Damond, please take this away. Damond, please take this away!"

Again, the pulling that would see him freed.

John Foreskin is helpless to watch. He knows he can only die. He knows he can only surrender. "Damond, please take this away!"

The pulling relents.

"NO!!!!!"

Don't abandon me! Please!

"Damond, please kill me, Damond!" John is yelling, his voice hoarse, but everyone around him is yelling, too.

The pulling stops.

"NOOO! PLEASE!" He wants to cry. But he can't.

And then, instead of the pull, he feels a sharp stab, and then a field of flux materializing within his torso, and then... a painful tingling. The gradual disintegration of the mass. He can feel it, breaking down into smaller and smaller parts, its hold on him steadily weakening, until finally

—a painful tug—

and the remnants are sucked out of him.

He chokes, gasping for air as a vacant agony escapes his mouth. His torso convulses. He covers his face. But the agony is gone now. And he feels only joy at the exiting of so much stagnant pain.

He doesn't know though...

He isn't sure....

He is...

He is not what has left him.

He probes the emptiness that remains for any sign... of its former tenant.

Nothing.

It is gone.

He is still himself.

But he isn't…

He isn't…

The Original Secret.

It has left him.

The mind he was tasked with carrying.

And John suddenly knows.

The last twenty-nine years of his life have reached their conclusion.

My job…

It has been my job to…

It's over now.

His mind falls silent. Everyone around him is still praying and wailing as before. Through bleary eyes, he looks up at the projector screen, and the silhouette of the man shifts.

He can feel me.

That is a real man.

And that man is the Owner of the Universe!

God bless you, Damond! Wherever you are, thank you! Thank you! Thank you!

John looks around as the first light of morning streaks through the curtains. He looks from face to face at all the people who have helped him…Dudek and Adam. Hyemin. The helpers from the other centers. His mind jumps to the first time he met le Kyle. Then to Kerry. And Dmitry. They've all helped him. They were all just doing their best. Just like he was.

Adam's voice cuts through the chaos, but now John feels its deep warmth.

He's only trying to help.

"BUK!

BUK!

BUK!

BUK!

BUK!

BUK!"

With eyes closed, John Foreskin searches again.

Nothing.

Nothing is there.

He only knows he feels tired. The world is…almost the same as it was. But he is… *himself*. Himself *again*, after what feels like a long, long time.

He tries again, this time giving up room for it to appear.   But there is only emptiness. An emptiness that used to be filled.

I'm finally alone.

He opens his eyes again, seeing everyone. They are all themselves. And they are all his brothers and sisters. He continues to cry.

25

The Final Post-Up

2018

"Bro."

"John Foreskin? Holy shit. Long time no see, man."

"You bleached your hair!"

"Yeah. Trying a new style."

"It's sick, man."

Is he going bald?

"Thanks. What have you been up to? Are you still…?"

"The Center? Nope. Haven't gone there in like, almost a year?"

"So you left shortly after I did. And Kerry?"

"You didn't hear? She went to the Main Center. Last I heard she was training to be a helper. By now they've probably got her at one of the local centers. She could be anywhere."

"No shit…Did you hear about Corey?"

"What about him?"

"He's got a kid now."

"You're kidding."

"Yeah man. I feel like my life has been on pause. Compared to some people our age, you know?"

"I feel you. I was wondering. You—."

"I what?"

"You kind of just disappeared."

"I ghosted you guys, eh?"

"Well, I guess everybody lost touch at the end."

"That's my bad, man. Well, I did what I had to do. So I won't apologize." Le Kyle swallows.

John follows their eyes up the street. "Where you heading?"

"Work actually. Wanna walk for a bit?"

"Sounds good."

"Smoke? Or did you quit?"

"I'll have one. Thanks."

The first exhalation unites the two millennials in an interracial siblinghood of consciousness. They walk side by side, and le Kyle doesn't feel as tall to John as they once did.

"If you don't mind me asking, I mean about you leaving, did it have anything to do with Kerry? You guys were at each other's throats back then."

"Huh? No. We ran hot and cold. But at bottom things were fine. Wait, did you think?"

"I mean, it crossed my mind."

"That's funny, bro. Nah. Nothing ever happened between Kerry and me." Le Kyle looks over at John.

"What is it?"

"I'm not sure, exactly. Your face has changed though. Your entire vibe kind of."

"Has it?"

"Yeah. You seem more comfortable in your own skin."

"Thanks. I mean, I do feel like I've changed."

"I'm happy for you, bro."

They walk a while in silence, down the crowded sidewalk of noonhour West Broadway, until le Kyle suddenly stops.

"You good?"

"I should tell you something."

"What is it?"

Le Kyle takes a deep breath. "The real reason why I just up and left. It wasn't really to do with the Center. It was because of shit between Dmitry and me. I mean—that's not all of it. But it's a big part."

"What kind of shit?"

"You know he and I used to be roommates, right? Before West 14ᵗʰ I mean. I'm the one who got him his room in the house."

"Right. Yeah."

"Well." Le Kyle's upper lip quivers. "We weren't just roommates. We were a couple."

John exhales. "Yo. I didn't know that—I mean—so what was the problem at the end?"

They start walking again.

"Basically, I wanted to focus on the Method, you know? I really believed in it. But I kept getting the feeling that Dmitry was there because of me. And at the time that seemed whack, you know? We had already broken up. We had even seen other people."

"Right. I get that. We were all so hardcore about the Center back then."

"Exactly."

John tries to laugh. "And I guess Dmitry did seem more casual about it. The Method, I mean."

"In a way, I feel bad for never telling you. Cuz we were pretty tight, and it was always this kind of wall between us. Especially considering that Kerry knew."

"Nah man. I get it."

"It was partly for Dmitry's sake. But mine, too, if I'm being honest. He pretty much had to live a lie in Russia. Dude hasn't even seen his family in like six years. So by default he 's pretty private about that stuff."

"Shit. I never even knew."

"Yeah man."

The two millennials walk in silence for a while longer.

"So, do you ever think you're gonna go back to the Center?" asks John.

"Bro." Le Kyle sighs, his shoulders relaxing "I mean. Sometimes I want to, but…my life was on pause because of that place, you know? And that whole *root* business? I mean. Maybe you found yours? But me? I already knew I was gay. You know what I mean? I have baggage and stuff. But they kept saying you need to *find your root,* and I'm there thinking, I already know myself. Which of course you're not supposed to think. So that just created all kinds of inner tension. And then at the Final Education, I felt like—like I didn't get what I was supposed to get out of it. It was kind of a huge letdown, if I'm being honest."

"I feel you."

They reach Broadway & Granville, one of John's old haunts.

"Post up here for a bit? I'm actually starting work in a few minutes."

"Wait, Starbucks?"

"Yeah man. This is my second job. We had it so good on West 14th. I'm in Yaletown now. It's fucking nuts what I'm paying for a place with two other dudes. And I'm in the living room, curtained off."

"That's crazy."

"Yeah. I needed to switch things up though."

John scuffs the ground with his shoe.

"You working though?"

"Tutoring part-time. Same as before."

"Enjoying it?"

"It's alright. Still trying to figure out what I want to do next."

"You've got time." Le Kyle checks his phone.

"Before you go in," says John, suddenly eager. "What's your take on those days? The Center I mean."

"Honestly, man? I don't know if Damond is a god. Or *god* himself. Or just, like, a really powerful shaman, you know what I mean? I felt things. We all did, right? Or else why would we have stayed? But was it because of Damond? I honestly don't know. Meditation is meditation. Maybe if you look inside of yourself long enough, you start to experience weird shit."

"True that."

"We were definitely in deep for a while. That's all I know."

"It's been weird adjusting," says John. "To life I mean. The longer I'm away from it, the more it all just feels like a distant memory, even though I know it changed me forever."

"Exactly," says le Kyle. "And yet somehow I'm back to my old ways."

"Exactly!"

John closes his eyes, breathing in, and the picture of his surroundings begins to fade.

"Alright, man," says le Kyle. "You have my number right? Or at least my email. I should get going though."

"Alright." John extends his hand. But somehow the bro shake turns into a bro hug, and after a second, John almost lets go, but he feels le Kyle's arms tighten.

"Take care of yourself, John. You deserve to be happy."

26

Nemesis: One in Six

2021

November. Practically Mormon, John Foreskin has not drunk coffee in six weeks. He goes out to the balcony to shiver and vape and look around at the whole wide world twenty-six floors below. Countless cars zoom past, implying countless lives and countless subjective experiences. People busy without regard for John. None of what he feels inside is down there. None of it is even inside the bare, off-white walls of his high-rise, fob-accessed, thus-far-afforded, live-in-girlfriend apartment.

The Center was right about that part, at least.

The Center. It feels like another lifetime. He hasn't talked to le Kyle or Kerry in years now. Everyone from that period just kind of slipped away. Now and then he'll receive a text, completely impersonal, linking him to the Center's website, or inviting him to a free seminar. He always clicks the link, and every time it's the same words that originally got him hooked.

Find your true mind: The Universe Mind
The Method
Free Introductory Seminar

It was a few months before John began returning to his old senses. After a week, he came down with something and was in bed for four days with sweats, muscle aches, and a fever. But when he came out the other side, he felt freer. Only after a full twelve months did he begin to feel like he'd made the right decision. He called it his thawing-out period.

He started working full time, then eventually returned to school. And he slowly began getting back in touch with the people he knew before he got so deep into the Method. With some of them, especially family, he began talking about the Original Secret, what the Center called his *root*. Talking helped. And when people asked him why he left the Center, he would tell them that he just kind of stopped going. The end was as unplanned as its fateful beginning, that day in the café when Dudek called his name.

On the bus to UBC every day, he thought of the Center. Little by little, it was losing its hold over him. And then one day after an exam, he decided to walk by. He didn't know why, and he wasn't nervous until he turned onto Balaclava Street and the house came into view.

He was walking in the middle of the street when his entire body seized up. It was Hyemin. She was on the front lawn, standing over somebody pulling weeds. Action meditation. John recognized the student, too. She'd been around, back in the day. Hyemin looked straight at him, her eyes like two black holes that conveyed no sign of recognition. John looked away first and kept on walking. Then he thought he heard the Center's front door open and began walking slightly faster, his entire body burning up. When he finally reached West Broadway, the hustle and bustle of rush hour made him feel safe again. The world was bigger than what went on in the Center. It was around that time that John felt like he'd finally finished thawing out, and around when he began to look forward, more so than backward, towards his future, and what adulthood might have in store for him

There are many things about adulthood that John Foreskin finds challenging. He isn't a racialized person, though he does possess human DNA. This sometimes gives him a sense of hopelessness when filling out on-line applications for government jobs and graduate programs. The heaviest counter-weight to his white male privilege—his being sexually molested at the age of four—is not represented in any of the application fields, not that he is particularly eager to disclose this detail of his formative years. He half hopes, but mostly doesn't, that one day this *section* of his identity will become politicized in the mainstream so that he can capitalize on it and land some kind of less precarious employment.

A firetruck passes below, sirens wailing, followed closely by a line of brawny cyclists.

I should be walking more.

At least John's sure he will do his pushups again today, a daily routine that brings him closer to the masculine ideal, however toxic. Soon he will have the upper-body strength to withstand the "buddy" greeting wielded by chads everywhere. It will become for him a gesture of universal brotherhood, rather than a subtle means of subordination.

Owing to his childhood run-in with the pedophile, John never completed the 10,000 hours of rough and tumble play that most of the other boys seemed to gravitate towards. Little John always stood on the outskirts, looking in on the bare limbs and gnashing teeth, wondering why the other boys were so eager to mix with each other, so eager to give things their all.

Why can I never give anything my all?

Maybe now I finally can.

This brings us again to the two goals that John confessed to the Universe back at his old place:

1. To live in my own apartment
2. To have an Asian girlfriend

He formulated these goals after watching some YouTube video about the law of attraction, and shortly after his Uncle Keith told him *"The world is your oyster."* He resisted at first because depression, because nihilism, and because he hated how Uncle Keith's generally good financial situation lent all of his casual advice an air of tried-and-true Boomer validity. Uncle Keith enjoys the adult dignity that comes with home ownership and disposable income, the same dignity that renters and lower-income people invariably have less of. He wears dress shirts underneath sweaters and reads the Economist. Who was John Foreskin to question his advice?

But now, several months later, both of John's goals have been achieved, though he has not yet grappled with the inherent patriarchal colonialism of his being particularly attracted to Asian women. For the time being, he allows this to dwell inside of him as a point of shame, regarding it as a kind of monstrous appetite, as opposed to a personal preference, or even the less palatable *acquired taste*. Perhaps in the future, following a family intervention, he will undergo exposure therapy in Utah and emerge with a healthy appetite for meat, potatoes, and Playboy Magazine.

As for the new apartment, it means that John no longer has to share a toilet seat with Mitch, the balding, obese, alcoholic, Caucasian male who owns three guns and watches YouTube videos about how the Bible foretold everything that is now going on between Israel and the Arab states. Living with Mitch in that basement suite[25] for three damp, stagnant years served as John's daily reminder of just how swimmingly his life was going after the Center.

You cannot fully convince John Foreskin that balding is not a disease and that it is not contagious. Nor can you fully convince him that balding is not cosmic punishment administered by Nemesis, the Greek goddess of divine retribution. Suffice it to say, the pedophile who adjusted the trajectory of John's life was a bald, Caucasian male.

Now, not having to share a bathroom—except with his Asian and female girlfriend whose flesh he hungers

---

[25] Standard dwelling of the Vancouver underclass

for—is huge. The pedophile custodian molested John in the daycare bathroom, and the bathrooms of John's Kafkaesque dreams are always doorless, windowed affairs with countless intrusive onlookers depriving John of his privacy when he really has to go.

His recent streak of immaculate poops coincides with his new private bathroom and his new habit of chain vaping. His main goal now is not graduate school, nor even the realization of life's meaning. His main goal is simply to afford his apartment because now he feels like he is one of the dignified adult Vancouverites, where dignity is defined as that air one acquires by using a fob key to enter one's apartment building and ride the elevator up to one's private sanctuary—the same dignity his Uncle Keith has in spades. Life now is about affording that sanctuary, where one watches YouTube, Twitch, and Netflix, and from where one orders Ubereats, Doordash, and Skipthedishes—all delivered by individuals somewhat less likely to be accruing dignity, as just now defined, but also less likely to be guilty of certain post-colonial sins, as wokely defined.

These days, when asked about the Center, John finds himself referring to it as a cult. And clearly, by some definitions, it is one. But John will never forget what that cult did for him. He can never forget the weight that was lifted, because from that moment on, in the registry of the Universe, John Foreskin has been living a lighter life.

The Center would say that he let go of falseness. John would say he has begun to live his *real* life. Maybe the reality or falseness of a thing has to do with whether it is within a human's power to hold onto it or let it go. Maybe those things one *chooses* to hold onto are only real for them, and in that strict sense, false. Maybe once those things are let go, they no longer exist. The Universe reclaims them, and their account rebalances. Maybe that is hubris, not letting go.

And if what happened to John all those years ago happens to one in six boys, then maybe Nemesis is more merciful than John originally thought. If she cannot prevent these things from happening (if not even the Abrahamic God can), then maybe she isn't punishing these boys, these men, for what they hold onto. Maybe she's patiently waiting, watching over them and all of the excess self-consciousness they've accumulated (pride and shame being two sides of the same coin), urging them to relinquish it, and rejoicing every time one of them lets even a small portion go.

Looking out at the whole wide world—Vancouver, the distant mountains, and infinity beyond— it suddenly occurs to John that envy has never been his default posture. It was one he adopted, and, therefore, one he can shed. John Foreskin looks up at the grey November sky and exhales watermelon-apple into a Universe that knows his heart.

Acknowledgements

This book would not have been possible without the help and support of many people. Thank you to Itoya at Book Palette for your accommodation and patience, and to JETDA Books for helping emerging authors like me. Thank you to Chell Li for designing and producing the front and back covers. Thank you to everyone who subscribed to *The Chronicles of John Foreskin* Substack. Thank you to A. Sidorenko for reading the very first drafts of several chapters back in 2018 and for encouraging me to continue. Thank you to John and Cathy for discussion and encouragement during the final drafts. Thank you to Grey Wolf, Henry's Mom, and Lily for feedback. Thank you to the SFU Writer's Club for enduring my antics and allowing me to share early drafts of certain chapters. Thank you to Louise for discussion of ideas over Christmas dinner at a hotel restaurant I never would have dined at on my own dime. (You visited so many times over the years that you probably don't know which dinner I'm referring to.) Thank you to S Wang for reading more than you ever had to, offering feedback, discussing ideas, and always encouraging me. Thank you to the editors: Skylar Brown for proofreading and developmental feedback, and Sa'ad Hassan for proofreading, extensive discussions over many hours, and assistance with revisions. Finally, thank you to Ayano for your patience, encouragement, and love.

If you enjoyed reading this book, please leave a review on the platform where you bought it.
I read every review and they help new readers discover this book.

~Thank you
N.G.

About the Author

Nick Guthry lives in Fukuoka with his wife and their twelve screens. In his spare time, he enjoys football (the kind Arsenal plays), riding his bicycle, chess, and PC games. Good Boy Alchemy is his first novel. For slightly more information, please visit nickguthry.com or look for him on social media.

Good
Boy
Alchemy

Confessions of a
White Cis Hetero Male

First Edition
ISBN 978-4-86753-744-2

Manufactured by Amazon.ca
Acheson, AB

12719671R00201